Alberta
Probate Kit

Lynne Butler, BA, LLB

Self-Counsel Press
(a division of)
International Self-Counsel Press Ltd.
Canada   USA

Self-Counsel Press acknowledges the financial support of the Government of Canada through the Canada Book Fund (CBF) for our publishing activities.

Printed in Canada.

First edition: 2011

Library and Archives Canada Cataloguing in Publication

Butler, Lynne

    Alberta probate kit / Lynne Butler.
    Includes guidebook, CD, and forms.

    ISBN 978-1-77040-069-6

    1. Probate law and practice — Alberta — Popular works. 2. Probate law and practice — Alberta — Forms. I. Title.

KEA246.A82B87 2010   346.712305'2   C2010-906879-3
KF765.Z9B87 2010

Self-Counsel Press
(a division of)
International Self-Counsel Press Ltd.

1481 Charlotte Road	1704 North State Street
North Vancouver, BC V7J 1H1	Bellingham, WA 98225
Canada	USA

Contents

Samples

Tables

Checklists

Introduction

You have been named the executor of an estate and you are wondering what steps you need to take. Or maybe someone close to you has passed away without a will and you are wondering what to do first. If so, you have come to the right place. This kit has been designed to help individuals deal with the estate of a family member or friend who has passed away, where the estate of the deceased person is in Alberta. It is designed for use by people who do not necessarily have any experience with wills, probate, or the courts, and offers step-by-step instructions.

This kit will help you apply for a Grant of Probate (if there is a will and you are the executor [or executrix if female] of the estate) or a Grant of Administration (if there is no will and you are the administrator of the estate). It will explain legal terms and tax terms, and it will guide you through each document you need to prepare and explain in detail how to use those documents to get the results you want from the courts.

This kit will also help you deal with the assets of the estate after you have obtained the Grant of Probate or Grant of Administration from the court. You will find out what steps to take first after a loved one has passed away, how to deal with the paperwork, and how to get assets into the hands of the beneficiaries.

You should use this kit if one of the following scenarios applies to you:

- You are the executor or one of the executors named in the will of someone who has passed away.

- Someone else is the first-named executor in a will, but that person cannot or will not act as executor and you are the alternate executor named.

- The person who died left a will, but the person named as executor cannot or will not act as executor and there is no alternate executor named, leaving the deceased person with a will but no executor to look after the estate.

- Someone has passed away, but no will can be found anywhere and you want to apply to be the administrator of the estate.

The person whose will you want to probate or whose estate you want to administer should have resided in Alberta at the time of his or her death. You apply in Alberta even if the death occurred while the person was temporarily out of Alberta, such as while on vacation or while working overseas.

If your goal is to contest a will or make a claim against an estate, this is not the right kit for you. Neither is it the right kit if you need to reseal a Grant of Probate from another jurisdiction.

While the kit gives some assistance with special situations such as handwritten wills, be sure to read Chapter 2, section **5.**, which discusses consulting a lawyer when you are in over your head. It is probably a mistake to try to probate a will yourself in certain circumstances, such as when a dispute is brewing, so read that section before starting.

This kit contains many handy checklists. You will find the checklists most helpful if you read the material in this book first, as it explains the terms used in the checklists and gives much more detail about the steps you must take.

Though you will find this kit is written in plain English, there are some legal terms that must be used.

To find the documents that you need to use, first decide which kind of application you want to make. The choices are:

- Application for probate: Do this if there is a valid will

- Application for administration: Do this if there is no will

- Application for administration with will annexed: Do this if there is a will but no executor (because the executor named has died or refuses to act)

The documents are separated into basic documents that are needed for EVERY application and specialized documents that you will only use in certain situations. Complete the basic documents first, then read through the list of specialized documents to see which ones apply to you. Each specialized document contains instructions about when to use it.

You will note that each of the documents you use in this kit contains a number beginning with the letters "NC" at the top right-hand corner, such as "NC8," as well as a title, such as "Affidavit of witness to a will." These numbers are assigned to the documents by the Surrogate Rules of Alberta and are used in this kit to ensure that your documents fulfill the legal requirements. They are also very handy for quickly checking that you have the right document. Do not remove these numbers.

The forms in this kit were made from precedent documents and set up in the way the courts have directed. Do not remove any words or parts of the documents unless you are instructed to do so.

If you are an executor or administrator and you have bought this book to help you with the job, you may be reimbursed for the purchase. Keep the receipt and include it as an out-of-pocket expense when you submit your final request for compensation, as set out in Chapter 19.

1

Things to Do Following the Death of a Loved One

In this chapter, you will find a list of things that you, as an executor, should be looking after when a loved one has passed away. Though they are not part of the Application for Probate, they are matters that fall under your responsibility. Do not wait for the Grant of Probate to be issued before you turn your attention to these items; all of them are matters that need attention earlier than that.

Matters are not quite as simple if you are applying for a Grant of Administration rather than a Grant of Probate. Unlike an executor, you do not have any legal right to handle the deceased's affairs until the court has issued your Grant of Administration. Once a Grant of Administration is issued, the administrator can act as executor even though he or she is called a different name.

1. Make Funeral Arrangements

It is the executor's job to make funeral, burial, or cremation arrangements, even when the executor is not the next of kin of the deceased. Most executors try to work with the family's wishes, but if the family is not agreed on what to do, the executor must make a decision. Check the will to see whether any arrangements have been pre-made or prepaid, and whether the deceased expressed any wishes. If the will does not say anything about it, the decision is up to the executor.

If you are not an executor but are applying to become an administrator, you do not have the same right as the executor in deciding what to do about the deceased's remains. The family members (next of kin) will make the decisions about burial, cremation, and other issues relating to the holding of a service. If you are the next of kin, you can go ahead and make arrangements without waiting for the Grant of Administration.

The bill for the funeral may be paid from the deceased's bank account, assuming there are sufficient funds. You can go to the bank and give the funeral bills (funeral home, flowers, obituary, lunch, etc.) to the banking officer and the bill will be paid directly to the funeral home. This is something that either an executor or an administrator can do.

When approaching a bank to pay the funeral bill, you will likely find it a smoother process if you can show a Certificate of Death or a Funeral Director's Statement of Death. If there is a will appointing you as executor, that will make it easier as well. If there is no will and you are applying to be an administrator, the bank may decide to refuse your request. If that happens, the funeral home may have no choice but to wait until the Grant of Administration is granted to you and you gain access to estate funds.

2. Banking Issues

You will have to go to the deceased's home early on to check for bills that are outstanding. Gather up phone, Internet, heat, water, cellphone, and any other bills you can find. Also look around for paperwork that will tell you about any mortgages or loans that are ongoing.

These bills may also be paid from the deceased's account as long as they are clearly bills of the deceased and as long as there are funds available. As mentioned in the previous section, this process is easier if you have a death certificate or Funeral Director's Statement of Death as well as a will that appoints you as executor.

At this point, do not worry about bills that are not urgent. You will be able to handle the bills more easily once you have your Grant of Probate or Grant of Administration. For now, you just want to make sure that no harm will come to the estate assets. For example, you do not want the heat to be turned off in a house in sub-zero weather, as that could cause damage to the house.

You may wish to open an executor's bank account at this time. It does not need to be at the same bank where the deceased held accounts; it can be at any bank. You may wish to get a bit more information before you do this. See section **10.** of this chapter for more on executors' bank accounts.

3.   Secure the House and Notify the Insurer

If the deceased lived alone in a house or condominium, make sure that nobody can enter. Change the locks if family members or neighbours have a key. You are responsible for every item in the home so make sure nothing goes missing.

Call the insurance company that provides homeowner's insurance to the deceased and let them know that the house is vacant. If you don't do this and there is damage due to a fire or burst pipes, for example, the coverage may be denied. This could leave you legally responsible for the loss.

Take valuables in the home into custody. There could be cash lying around, credit cards, identification cards, or jewelry. There could also be larger valuable items such as antiques or artwork. Everything must be kept in a secure location under your control, such as a safety deposit box.

If the deceased lived in a rented apartment, tell the landlord about the death immediately. Ask that the locks be changed if possible. Secure all valuables as described above. Remember that you must pay the rent on the apartment until you can arrange for everything in it to be sold or distributed and for the apartment to be cleaned. This may take several weeks.

4.   Check the Safety Deposit Box

You will hopefully be able to find out where the deceased person banked by looking through the papers you find in his or her home. Once you know which branches of which banks you are dealing with, go to the branches and ask to see any safety deposit box the deceased might have rented. Be prepared to show the following:

- A notarized copy of the will showing that you are named as the executor;
- A Certificate of Death or Funeral Director's Statement of Death confirming the death of the deceased; and
- Your personal identification.

As you are unlikely to gain access to the safety deposit box without a will that proves you have a legal right to make the enquiry, only an executor will be able to do this before getting the grant. An administrator will have to wait until a Grant of Administration has been issued.

Once you gain entry to the safety deposit box, make a detailed list of the items in the box. You do not have to remove them right now, but it is important that you know what is there. Some of the items might have to be listed on your Application for Probate.

5. Find the Original Will

To apply for a Grant of Probate, you must have the original signed will, not a photocopy. Any family member, lawyer, or banker who has the original must turn it over to you once you have proof of the death of the deceased, as it is your legal right and obligation to carry out the wishes in the will. Read Chapter 4 to find out whether the will is valid.

The original will is going to be given to the court in the Application for Probate, so make copies of the will as soon as you get it. As you progress through your duties as executor, you will notice that many people at banks, registries, and other places will ask you for a notarized copy of the will, so it is best if you get several copies notarized.

6. Get Copies of the Death Certificate

There are two types of certificates available to you, and they fill similar but not identical roles. You can choose one or both. Most executors and administrators will request one original death certificate and several original Funeral Director's Statement of Death. A Certificate of Death is issued by the Province of Alberta through a registry agent. They currently cost $20 per certificate. If you place an order, you will get only one original certificate unless you specify otherwise. It is usually not available immediately as it can only be produced once the province receives and processes information from the funeral director, coroner, or the hospital where the deceased died.

A Funeral Director's Statement of Death is issued by the funeral home that processed the deceased. Most funeral homes will provide the executor with at least three or four copies of the Funeral Director's Statement of Death and the cost is included in the cost of the funeral. You do not have to make a special request for this document, as it is part of the legal responsibility of the funeral director to document each funeral or cremation.

For most purposes having to do with gathering in the assets of an estate, you can decide whether you want to use a Death Certificate or a Funeral Director's Statement of Death as proof of death. Because Death Certificates are more expensive, executors will often choose to save costs and use a Funeral Director's Statement of Death instead. In the majority of situations, this will be adequate. There are a few places that will insist upon the government-issued death certificate, the most notable of which is the Land Titles Office.

When you are dealing with banks, investment houses, insurance companies, and most other places, you have the option of providing a notarized copy of the document rather than parting with one of your scarce originals. The most cost-efficient system is to get a Funeral Director's Statement of Death, make several photocopies, and have them notarized.

7. Have the Deceased's Mail Redirected to You

Go to a Canada Post location and fill in the form that instructs them to forward all of the deceased's mail to you. Keep the receipt for reimbursement from the deceased's estate later.

8. Place an Obituary in the Newspaper

An obituary is not required by law, but it is customary. Normally it is placed in the paper in time to allow friends and associates to attend the funeral service. Keep the receipt for reimbursement from the estate later.

9. Notify Various Parties of the Death of the Deceased and Cancel Coverage

There are numerous people and places that you must notify of the death of the deceased. Most executors find that it is easier to go in person where possible. Very few places will accept this information by telephone. Depending on the circumstances of the deceased's life, you will likely have to notify the following:

- Alberta Health Care
- Blue Cross
- Life insurance company
- Home insurance company
- Vehicle insurance company
- Motor vehicles registry
- Employer
- Employer health plan
- Landlord
- Canada Revenue Agency
- Old Age Security
- Canada Pension Plan

- Veterans' Affairs
- Private pensions from employers or previous employers
- Assured Income for the Severely Handicapped (AISH) program
- Banks and credit card companies
- Investment advisors
- Newspapers and magazine subscriptions
- Doctor's office
- Telephone company
- Cellphone company
- Internet company
- Cable TV company
- Utilities provider

A sample letter for letting interested non-family parties know that the deceased has died is included in Sample 1 and on the CD. The letter contains various paragraphs for you to choose from (for example, if you wish to request that coverage of some kind be discontinued). You will notice that some letters require a notarized copy of the will and a notarized copy of either the death certificate or the Funeral Director's Certificate of Death. You should also expect to provide these copies when you give notice in person. Do not release the original will to anyone other than the court; nobody else needs the original even though they may ask you for it.

10. Open an Executor's Bank Account

You should open a new bank account in your name in trust for the estate. For example:

John Smith, in trust for the Estate of Joan Smith

or

The Estate of Joan Smith (with you as the authorized signatory)

You can do this either where you bank or where the deceased banked. Into this account you will deposit any cheques you receive that are payable to the deceased or to his or her estate. For example, you may have a cheque come in for a refund of a prepaid subscription to a newspaper. When you get the CPP death benefit, you will deposit that. You will also deposit any cash you find in the deceased's home. Whenever an asset (for example, the deceased's car) is sold, deposit the money into this account.

Sample 1
Letter Advising of Death and Cancelling Coverage

_____
Your name
_____
_____
Your address

Date

Name
Address

Dear _____:

Re: The Estate of _____, Deceased
      Account Number: _____

I am the executor of the estate of _____, who passed away on
_____. I am writing to you to let you know of his/her
passing. I am enclosing a notarial copy of the Funeral Director's Statement of Death for
your records.

(Choose one or more of the following paragraphs, as fits your needs:)

- Please amend your records.
- Please discontinue service immediately and send the final bill to me.
- Please discontinue service immediately. I understand there will be a refund. Please
  forward a cheque payable to The Estate of _____ to me.
- Please transfer the account into the name of _____.
- Please let me know what steps need to be taken to close the account, and provide me
  with any forms I will need.

Yours truly,

_____
(Your name)

If the deceased was receiving Old Age Security benefits, Canada Pension Plan retirement benefits, or any other public pension, the estate is entitled to keep the cheque that was issued for the month in which the deceased died. Any benefits that are for later months must be returned.

As the settlement of the estate progresses, you will have other monies to put into this account. You may have the proceeds of insurance policies, the sale of the deceased's home, or of an RRSP. Use this account to process and hold all funds that are intended for the estate.

You will also pay bills from the account. If, in the early stages of the estate, there are no estate funds available and you end up using your own money to pay bills, you are entitled to be reimbursed from this account for these payments before any beneficiaries receive their shares. Keep your receipts to back up your accounting of what you believe you spent. Later on, you will pay the beneficiaries their shares of the estate from this account.

It is absolutely essential that you keep this money separate from your own funds. Never mingle the deceased's money with anyone else's. Do not make this account joint with anyone other than a co-executor who is also actively working on the estate.

11. Apply for CPP Death Benefit

The Canada Pension Plan (CPP) pays a sum of money to the executor or administrator of the estate of a person who has passed away to be used to pay estate expenses, particularly the funeral bill. The benefit will not be paid out automatically, so you must apply for it on behalf of the estate. The form shown in Sample 2 is available online at www.servicecanada.gc.ca, from CPP offices, and from most funeral homes.

Anyone who has had a CPP deduction taken off his or her paycheques is eligible to receive a death benefit. Currently, the maximum amount payable to an estate is $2,500.

Depending on the deceased's circumstances, there may be other benefits, such as a survivor benefit or survivor allowance, that are available. Applying for these other benefits is not the executor's job, because they are paid to family members, not to the estate.

Sample 2 shows the first page of the CPP Death Benefit Application.

Sample 2
CPP Death Benefit Application Form

Service Canada

Protected when completed - B

Personal Information Bank HRSDC PPU 146

Application for a Canada Pension Plan Death Benefit

It is very important that you:

- send in this form with supporting documents (see the information sheet for the documents we need); **and**
- use a **pen** and **print** as clearly as possible.

DO NOT COMPLETE THE SHADED AREAS

SECTION A - INFORMATION ABOUT THE DECEASED

FOR OFFICE USE ONLY

1A. Social Insurance Number	1B. Date of Birth Year Month Day	1C. Country of Birth (If born in Canada, indicate province or territory)	AGE ESTABLISHED
			AA

2A. Sex ☐ Male ☐ Female	2B. Date of Death *(See the information sheet for a list of acceptable proof of date of death documents)* Year Month Day	ESTABLISHED DATE OF DEATH	PROV. CODE
			AA

3. Marital status at the time of death
(See the information sheet for important information about marital status)

☐ Single ☐ Married ☐ Separated

☐ Common-law ☐ Surviving spouse or common-law partner ☐ Divorced

SURNAME - VALIDATOR

AR

4A. ☐ Mr. ☐ Mrs. Usual First Name and Initial   Last Name
☐ Ms. ☐ Miss

4B. Name at birth, if different from 4A. (e.g. maiden name, legal name change, etc.)   First Name and Initial   Last Name

4C. Name on social insurance card, if different from 4A.   First Name and Initial   Last Name

5. Home Address at the time of death (No., Street, Apt., R.R.)   City

Province or Territory   Country other than Canada   Postal Code

6A. If the address shown in number 5 is outside of Canada, indicate the province or territory in which the deceased last resided.	6B. In which year did the deceased leave Canada?

7. Did the deceased ever live or work in another country? ☐ No ☐ Yes ▶ **If yes,** indicate the names of the countries and insurance numbers. (If you need more space, use the space provided on page 4 of this application). Also, indicate whether a benefit has been requested.

	Country	Insurance Number	Has a benefit been requested?
a)			☐ Yes ☐ No
b)			☐ Yes ☐ No
c)			☐ Yes ☐ No

Service Canada delivers Human Resources and Skills Development Canada programs and services for the Government of Canada.

Disponible en français

SC ISP1200 (2009-11-013) E   Page 1 of 4   Canada

2

Grant of Probate

1. What Is Probate?

"Probate" is the process of submitting the original will of a deceased person to the court and obtaining a Grant of Probate from the court. Essentially, to probate a will means to prove it's real. The package of documents that you send to the court is called an Application for Probate. A Grant of Probate is an order of the court that confirms in writing the validity of the will and the authority of the executor. The Grant of Probate is court authority for the executor, the beneficiaries, and everyone else affected in some way by the will to carry out the wishes of the deceased person as described in the will.

A Grant of Probate is obtained by submitting to the court a package of documents that includes the original will, sworn evidence that the will was properly executed, a list of all the assets and debts of the deceased, information about the deceased's family, and a court fee. The executor is responsible for gathering and submitting this package. It is not necessary to appear in front of a Justice of the Court of Queen's Bench of Alberta as long as your package of information is complete and accurate, and as long as the Justice is satisfied that there are no issues that need to be sorted out.

2. Do I Need Probate?

Not every will must go through the probate process. However, if the deceased person owned assets in his or her own name, there is a very good chance that probate will be required. Look at the assets in the estate with the following in mind.

Probate is not required to deal with:

- Property that the deceased owned as joint owner with another person, such as real estate or a bank account, as those assets will automatically belong to the other joint owner by right of survivorship.

- Assets that name a beneficiary directly, such as a life insurance policy or an RRSP that names someone other than the person's estate.

Probate is always required when the deceased person owned real estate (including homes, cottages, raw land, or mineral interests) in his or her name alone. When determining whose name is on the title to real property, always go to the Land Titles Office and ask for a title search. Do not assume that because the family always thought of a parcel of land as belonging to someone that it necessarily does belong to that person, or to him or her alone. Always check the title.

Probate is almost always required when there are registered assets such as Registered Retirement Savings Plans (RRSPs), Registered Retirement Income Funds (RRIFs), Locked-In Retirement Accounts (LIRAs), or others that name the estate as the beneficiary. Even bank accounts and non-registered investments over a certain amount (which varies from bank to bank) may mean that you need to get probate. Few banks will release more than about $10,000 without probate.

If you are not sure if you need to apply for probate, you can ask a lawyer. Alternatively, you may determine which asset of the estate is the largest and make a few calls. For example, if the deceased died leaving no house but a RRIF and an account at a certain bank, call that bank and ask about their requirements. Requirements for releasing funds and accessing account information vary from bank to bank and branch to branch.

3. How Long Will It Take?

You cannot make your application to the court until at least seven days have passed since the deceased person died.

Then it usually takes several weeks of investigation and work before you can finish your documents. The inventory, in particular, can take a long time to prepare because you may be waiting for information from banks, brokers, Land Titles Office, insurance companies, or other sources.

Once your application is filed with the court, you should expect to wait four to six weeks for it to be processed and the Grant of Probate to be sent to you. Keep in mind that if you make mistakes in your application or leave out information, the Clerk of the Court might reject your documents and require you to fix them and refile. This would start the clock running again from the beginning.

4. What Does It Cost?

When you file your Application for Probate or Application for Letters of Administration, you will have to pay a fee to the court. The fees are the same everywhere in Alberta and are based on the net value of the estate as shown on the inventory you completed. There is no GST added to the fees.

The court fees are:

Value of Estate	Court Fee
• $10,000 or under	$25
• over $10,000 but not more than $25,000	$100
• over $25,000 but not more than $125,000	$200
• over $125,000 but not more than $250,000	$300
• over $250,000	$400

The court fee described here includes all of the documents that together make up an Application for Probate. Once you pay the fee, you do not have to pay again to file additional documents such as affidavits or releases.

However, there are separate (extra) fees for certain services such as filing a caveat or requesting photocopies. At the time of writing, the court charges the following fees:

Service Requested	Fee
• For each caveat filed	$200
• For each certified copy of a document other than the initial certified copy	$10
• For each search	$10
• For each page photocopied or faxed	$1

5. Can I Do This without a Lawyer?

If you are the executor of an estate, and the will, the assets, and the family situation are all straightforward, you should be able to complete the Application for Probate yourself without hiring a lawyer. Be honest with yourself here. If matters are too complicated for you to handle on your own or become too complicated halfway through, get a lawyer or trust company to help you.

Some of the situations in which you might be wise to consult a lawyer are where:

- someone in the family is determined to contest the will because he or she believes that the deceased person was pressured into writing the will in somebody's favour;

- someone in the family is claiming that he or she is entitled to more of the estate than he or she is going to get under the will;

- parts of the will can be read two ways, so you are not really sure what the deceased meant by it;

- words or sentences have been crossed out of the will, or words have been handwritten in between the lines;

- the will is not signed, not dated or not witnessed properly;

- you can only find a photocopy of the will and not the original;

- the deceased owned assets in another country; or

- the deceased owned a house in his or her own name but the spouse wants to keep living there.

6. What Do Lawyers Charge to Obtain a Grant of Probate?

In Alberta, there is no set fee limit that lawyers can charge a client for obtaining a Grant of Probate. However, there has been a suggested fee guideline in place for about 15 years, and many lawyers choose to follow it. According to the guideline, a lawyer may charge $2,250 plus 0.5 percent of the gross value of the estate. If the estate is worth more than $150,000, the lawyer may charge $2,250 plus 1 percent of the gross value of the estate.

It is important to realize that this is not the lawyer's fee for administering the entire estate. This is only the fee for what is known as core legal services, which are only part of the job the executor needs to carry out. Core legal services include getting the Grant of Probate and all of the investigation and information gathering required to prepare the application. If you want the lawyer to do any non-core work, you must pay the lawyer his or her usual hourly rate in addition to the amount paid according to the formula set out in the previous paragraph.

Non-core legal services include keeping/preparing financial records for the estate, transferring assets to the beneficiaries, paying the estate's bills, and defending the estate against challenges.

7. How Do I Know If the Will Is Valid?

As an executor, you will be presenting the will to the court and swearing under oath that this is the valid last will and testament of the deceased. This means you have an obligation to make sure that you have found the right will and that it is valid. See Chapter 3 about reading and interpreting the will before you begin your process of applying for probate.

8. What Does an Executor Do?

There are various arrangements of executors possible under a will. Some wills appoint more than one executor, known as co-executors or joint executors. In this arrangement, both executors are equally responsible for the estate. Both of you will have to sign the Application for Probate and swear the affidavits. All decisions must be jointly made.

Another possible arrangement is that there is only one executor named, but if this person is not available or willing to be the executor, a second choice or alternate executor is named. In this case, the alternate executor has no say at all in how the estate is run unless the first-named executor is completely out of the picture. This might be the case if the first-named executor has passed away, has lost mental capacity, or has simply refused to be the executor.

If you are the alternate executor, you will have to explain in your Application for Probate why you are applying instead of the first-named executor. We will cover this in more detail in the instructions for completing the application document in Chapter 5.

The duties of an executor are extensive. Basically, the executor is the person responsible for making sure that every part of the estate is properly dealt with. There is quite a bit of detail, and some of the tasks you have to take on might be unfamiliar to you. At the end of this chapter and on the CD, you will find a checklist of executor's duties that you should use to keep track of what you have completed and what is still outstanding.

You should always be aware that as an executor, you have a fiduciary duty to the estate and to the beneficiaries. This means you are accountable to the estate and the beneficiaries for all of the property that passes through your hands, and you always have to behave in their best interests.

Most executors do not realize that if they make mistakes that cause a financial loss to the estate, they can be held personally liable for those mistakes. This means they might have to repay the losses out of their own money. As a general rule, an executor who is being honest and careful will not get into that kind of trouble.

9. What Do I Do about an Executor Who Doesn't Want to Take Part?

As mentioned earlier, there could be an executor named in a will who is not able to do the executor's job, or for some reason simply does not want to do it. An executor who is not going to accept the job is said to be renouncing his or her right to be the executor. If this happens when there are co-executors, the executor who is going to apply for the probate must have written indication from the co-executor who is renouncing. Form NC12, Renunciation of Probate, is the form for renouncing and is available in Chapter 6 and on the CD.

The signed renunciation must be included in your Application for Probate. Otherwise, the judge will be faced with a will that says there are two executors and an application signed by only one, and will consider that to be a mistake. The renunciation explains the situation.

This also happens when there is a first-choice executor and an alternate executor. If you are the alternate executor and you are applying for probate, you have to explain why the first-named person is not the one who is applying. If he or she chose to renounce, you have to let the court know by including the renunciation form in your Application for Probate.

The important thing to understand about choosing to renounce the right to be an executor is that it can only be done at the very beginning. A person is not allowed to start work as an executor then just walk away without finishing the estate. If there is a reason why the person cannot finish the job, such as becoming very ill, he or she has to ask the court for permission to stop being an executor. Once you start, you are an executor for life or until the court gives you permission to stop.

Once a person renounces the right to apply for probate or administration, he or she cannot change his or her mind unless the renunciation document specifically says that he or she reserves that right.

10. Am I the Right Person to Apply for Probate?

If you are an executor named in the will, you apply for a Grant of Probate. Only an executor (or group of executors) named in a will can apply for a Grant of Probate. But as we have just seen, sometimes an executor renounces his or her right to be the executor. If this happens and nobody who is named as executor is able and willing to be the executor, things change.

Anyone else who wants to use that will to look after the deceased's estate will apply for a Grant of Letters of Administration with Will Annexed. Though this is an intimidating title, it basically means permission to probate a will that has no executor. There is a section on this in Chapter 3. If no family members or beneficiaries are willing to act as administrator and there are assets that need to be dealt with, in rare cases the Office of the Public Trustee may step forward and apply to administer the estate.

11. Do I Need to Get a Bond?

A bond is a form of insurance policy purchased by an executor or administrator personally (that is, using his or her own money, not the estate's money). Its purpose is to ensure that the executor or administrator carries out the duties of the estate honestly and accurately. If the executor should defraud or neglect the estate, he or she will lose the money used to buy the bond. If the executor or administrator properly carries out all of his or her duties, the money will be returned to him or her.

In Alberta, the requirement for a bond is set out in the Surrogate Rules that govern all probate and estate matters.

You DO need to apply to an insurance company for a bond if:

- you are the only executor and you live outside of Alberta; or
- you are one of two or more executors and all of you live outside of Alberta.

You do NOT have to apply for a bond if:

- you are the only executor and you live in Alberta;
- you are a co-executor and at least one of the co-executors lives in Alberta; or
- you are applying to dispense with bond in your Application for Probate.

12. Recap of Executor's Duties

Take a moment and go over Checklist 1, Executor's Duties. This check-list is also available on the CD that accompanies this kit.

Checklist 1
Executor's Duties

Item	Done?	Chapter
Arrange for the funeral, cremation, service, etc.		1
Pay urgent bills.		1
Secure the deceased's home and notify the insurer that it's vacant.		1
Give notice of termination of lease to a landlord, if the deceased was renting a home.		1
Arrange for the protection and supervision of vacant land and buildings.		1
List the contents of every safety deposit box.		1
Find the original will.		1
Check the will for validity.		3
Get copies of the death certificate.		1
Have the deceased's mail redirected.		1
Place an obituary in the newspaper.		1
Find the deceased's insurance policies and notify each insurer of the death.		1
Place additional insurance on property if necessary.		1
Secure all estate property.		1
Provide for the proper management of any business operations of the deceased.		1
Cancel Old Age Security and Canada Pension Plan retirement benefits.		1
Cancel Alberta Health Care and any private health coverage such as Blue Cross.		1
Cancel the deceased's driver's license.		1
Cancel utilities, subscriptions, television, memberships, etc.		1
Open an executor's bank account.		1

Apply for the Canada Pension Plan death benefit.		1
Apply for any other pensions, annuities, death benefits, life insurance, or other benefits that are payable to the estate.		1, 16
Hire a lawyer to advise you on the administration of the estate, if necessary, or to bring any matter that is required to be heard before the court.		2
Apply for a Grant of Probate or Grant of Administration.		4 (Probate), 8 (Administration)
Make a list of all the beneficiaries of the estate, with names, addresses, and ages.		5 (Probate), 9 (Administration)
Compile a list of all real property and personal property of the deceased, including descriptions, locations, and values. Contact financial institutions, insurance companies, etc., to find out about balances.		7
For each piece of property, list any mortgages, leases, or other encumbrances against the property.		7
If the deceased was employed, contact the employer to advise of death and find out about any unpaid wages or death benefit.		7
Compile a list of all of the deceased's debts.		7
Notify charities of charitable bequests.		12
Notify beneficiaries of their inheritances.		12
Notify the Public Trustee if there is a minor or a missing person involved in the estate.		12
Notify spouses and former spouses of the deceased of your application.		12
Decide whether to advertise for claimants, check all claims, and make payments as funds become available.		13
Take the steps necessary to finalize an amount payable if the amount of a debt is an issue.		13
Set up a ledger and record all financial transactions for the estate.		14
Pay debts of the deceased.		13, 14

Close bank accounts, cash out investments, and transfer those funds to the executor's account.		15
Transmit real estate from the deceased into the name of the estate.		15
Sell estate property where applicable.		15
Advise any joint tenants of the death of the deceased.		16
Advise any designated beneficiaries of their interests under life insurance policies or other property passing outside the will.		16
Determine the income tax or other tax liability of the deceased and of the estate.		17
File tax returns on behalf of the deceased and the estate and pay any tax owing.		17
Obtain a Tax Clearance Certificate before distributing the estate property.		17
Hire an accountant to help with taxes.		17
Determine how much you should be paid as executor or administrator, and compile expenses.		18
Prepare Statement of Proposed Executor's (or Administrator's) Compensation.		19
Prepare Statement of Receipts and Disbursements.		19
Prepare Statement of Proposed Distribution.		19
Prepare a release for each residuary beneficiary.		19
Obtain releases from beneficiaries.		19
Pay specific gifts to charities and beneficiaries.		20
Set up any trusts directed by the will.		20
Distribute your financial statements to the residuary beneficiaries.		19, 20
Distribute household goods and personal items.		20
Once releases are obtained, pay yourself the agreed amount.		19
Pay the beneficiaries their shares.		20

3

Confirm That the Will Is Valid

If you are the executor, once you have located the will you intend to probate, you must read and examine it carefully before you take any steps. The same applies to any codicil (a separate document that amends a will) that is being probated. Remember that when you submit your package of documents to the court, you will be swearing an affidavit that this is the right will and that it is fit to be probated, so you must ensure that your sworn evidence is true. You also want to make sure that you understand the instructions given in the will right from the start so that you know what you are getting into.

Checklist 2 (also on the CD) is called the Will Review Checklist. You can use it to keep track of your steps, and the sections below explain what you should be looking for when examining the will. The sections correspond with the checklist. If you are probating both a will and a codicil, use a separate checklist for each document.

Codicils are used to change wills because they are shorter, quicker to make, and cheaper than making whole new wills. You will know that a will and codicil belong together because the first line of the codicil identifies the will it amends by date. Remember that you cannot choose to leave off a codicil (if one exists) and only probate the will. You are required to submit both documents.

Checklist 2
Will Review Checklist

Item	Yes	No	Follow-up Steps
The will is the original.			
The will is the most recent one.			
All pages appear to be present.			
The will is signed by the deceased.			
The will is dated.			
The will is witnessed by two people.			
One or both witnesses are also beneficiaries in the will.			
The deceased married after the date of the will.			
You are the named executor.			
There is a co-executor.			
There is an executor or co-executor who wants to renounce executorship.			
There are handwritten changes to the will.			
There is an Affidavit of Witness to a Will attached, and it is signed, dated, and commissioned.			
The back of the will is stamped as "Exhibit A."			
The will was signed in Alberta.			
There is a survivorship clause.			
The will states how much you will be paid to be the executor.			

1.   Is This the Original Will?

The Application for Probate must contain the original will of the deceased, whether it is a formal (typewritten) will or a holograph (handwritten) will. If the will you have is an original document, skip to the next item. If you have searched everywhere and cannot find the original, take the photocopy to a wills and estates lawyer and ask for assistance with your application.

2. Is This the Latest Will?

Check the date on the will. Most have a date included on the last page, right above the signature. Some have the date at the top of the first page. Every will and codicil should be dated, in large part to establish which of the possible existing wills is most recent.

A person's valid will is always the most recent one they made. Each time a new will is made, it completely revokes any earlier ones. Note that a codicil does not revoke a will, as it is designed to become part of a will. If there are both a will and a codicil in place and the testator made a new will, it revokes the earlier will and codicil. Always remember that the newest document is always the one that must be probated.

If the will is undated, this is problematic, especially if more than one will exists. It is not insurmountable, however. If the will is not dated, see what you can find that might help establish when the will was made. For example, there might be a letter or a bill from a lawyer that relates to the making of the will. The date on the letter might help establish the approximate date the will was made. Once you have that extra evidence in hand, take the will and your evidence to a wills lawyer to figure out whether the will can be probated.

3. Are All the Pages Accounted for?

If the pages of the will (and codicil, if applicable) are numbered, check to see that all pages are there. If the pages are not numbered but the paragraphs are numbered, follow the numbering pattern to make sure everything is in place. If there is no numbering at all, read the last sentence of each page to see whether it makes sense when it carries over to the top of the following page.

4. Did the Deceased Marry after Making the Will?

If the deceased person married after the date on the will, then the will is void and you cannot submit it to the court for probate. The only way the will is still valid is if it contains a clause, usually at the very beginning, that states that the will was made in contemplation of marriage to the person that the deceased did actually marry.

Living with someone in a common-law relationship that started after the will was made does not make the will void.

5. Is It Signed?

Every will and codicil, whether formal or handwritten, must be signed by the testator. If the will you have has been signed at the end by the deceased, skip to the next item. If not, read below.

Most people sign with their usual signature, but occasionally a person will sign using an "X." A will like that can still be probated, but you'll be required to follow specific rules regarding validating the signature. It is best if you consult a lawyer for help.

If the will is not signed at all, you have a problem. If you believe it to be the will that the deceased intended to leave, take it to an experienced wills and estates lawyer for advice on what, if anything, can be done.

6. If Holograph, Is It Completely in the Deceased's Handwriting?

Alberta's *Wills Act* recognizes wills that are "wholly in the handwriting of the deceased" as holograph wills. However, many people have used kits or Internet downloads to prepare wills, and some of those are a mix of typed and handwritten words. They do not qualify as holograph wills as they are not wholly in handwriting. In cases like that, you must treat the will not as a holograph, but as a formal will. This affects the witnessing requirements, as you will see in the next section.

7. Is It Witnessed by Two People?

Witnessing requirements apply only to formal wills; that is, wills that have been printed out from a computer or word processor. Wills that are handwritten do not need any witnesses, so if you are dealing with a handwritten will, you may skip to the next item.

A formal will must be signed by the deceased in front of two witnesses, and those two witnesses must then sign in front of the deceased and in front of each other. The will should contain a statement next to the deceased's signature that says, "Signed by _____ as his/her will in our presence and in the presence of each other," or some variation of this. Check that this clause is in the will and check that there are two witness signatures.

You should be able to identify who the witnesses are, either by reading the signatures themselves or because the names could be printed below the signatures.

8. Are the Witnesses Named as Beneficiaries in the Will?

A will may not be witnessed by:

- anyone who is a beneficiary of the will; or
- anyone whose spouse (married or common law) is a beneficiary of the will.

If one of the prohibited people has signed as a witness, the will itself is still valid and you should still send it to probate. However, the gift to the witness is not valid so the witness will not receive anything under the will. You will have to describe the situation on your Form NC6. If you are not entirely sure whether a beneficiary has signed as a witness, take the will to an estate lawyer for assistance.

9. Are You Named as the Executor?

Read the will carefully to make sure you understand who is appointed as executor. Are you appointed as the only executor or is there a co-executor named? If there is a co-executor, you both have to act jointly on all decisions and you both have to sign all paperwork.

Is anyone renouncing his or her right to be executor? This could be a co-executor who does not want to act or someone named before you who cannot or will not act. If there is anyone who is renouncing, make sure you read section **2.** in Chapter 6 so that you know what paperwork you must have in place.

10. Are There Any Handwritten Additions to the Will or Anything Crossed Out?

If the will appears to have words added to it after it was signed, in handwriting between the lines or scribbles in the margins, or if it appears that words have been crossed out, you should take the will to a lawyer. If you try to decide for yourself what is valid and what is not when the will has been modified this way, you may find that disappointed beneficiaries will blame you for their loss.

11. Is There a Form NC8 Affidavit of Witness to a Will Attached?

There are rules about how a will must be witnessed. In order for a judge to know that the rules were properly followed and the will is therefore valid, the judge looks at a document called Form NC8 Affidavit of witness to a will. If you are probating a formal will, this document is hopefully already attached to the will.

With older wills, the NC8 Affidavit is not always attached. If it is not, you will have to arrange for one to be prepared, sworn, and attached to the will. Read section **8.** in Chapter 5 for instructions on how to do that. This applies to formal wills only, and not to holograph wills.

12. Is the Back of the Will Stamped "Exhibit A"?

This is for formal wills only. The Form NC8 Affidavit of witness to a will contains a sentence that says the original will is attached as Exhibit A. Look on the back of the last page of the will, on which the deceased has signed. You should see a stamp that says:

This is Exhibit A to the Affidavit of
_____, sworn before me
at the City of _____, in the

_____
Province of Alberta, this _____ day
of _____.

_____
A Commissioner for Oaths in and for the
Province of Alberta

13. Is There a Survivorship Clause?

A survivorship clause gives instructions as to how long after the death of a deceased a person must live in order to inherit something under the will. Look for a clause that says something like, "A beneficiary must survive me by 30 days," or "If my spouse survives me by 20 days … "

When this type of clause is present, you cannot send your Application for Probate to the court until the survivorship time has expired. The time starts running on the day after the deceased's death.

4

How to Apply for the Grant of Probate

In this kit, the forms needed to apply for a Grant of Probate are divided into two main sections. The first section, which is covered in Chapter 5, includes the forms that are required on every Application for Probate. The second section, in Chapter 6, contains forms that are not always needed every time. I refer to these documents as the specialized forms. You may need some of them in your Application for Probate, depending on the circumstances of the estate on which you are working.

It is recommended that you read this chapter in full before attempting to complete the forms described in Chapter 5.

If you are applying for a Grant of Administration, proceed to Chapter 8.

1. Forms Needed

To apply for a Grant of Probate, you will need to prepare a package of documents for the court, all of which together make up your Application for Probate. Each one has to be tailored to the estate you are working on. The following forms are required in EVERY Application for Probate:

- Form NC1 — Application by the personal representative for a grant of probate

- Form NC2 — Affidavit by the personal representative(s) on application for a grant of probate

- Form NC3 — Schedule 1: Deceased

- Form NC4 — Schedule 2: Will

- Form NC5 — Schedule 3: Personal representative(s)

- Form NC6 — Schedule 4: Beneficiaries

- Form NC7 — Schedule 5: Inventory of property and debts

- Form NC8 — Affidavit of witness to a will

- Form NC19 — Notice to beneficiaries (residuary)

- Form NC27 — Affidavit of service

You will also need the original will. Note that if you are also probating a codicil, you will have to include a separate Form NC4 for the codicil as well as the original codicil itself. This is the only form that needs to be duplicated, as all other forms can refer to both the will and the codicil.

Other documents (the specialized forms discussed more in Chapter 6) that you may need depending on the circumstances are:

- Form NC9 — Affidavit of handwriting of deceased

- Form NC12 — Renunciation of probate

- Form NC17 — Affidavit to dispense with a bond

- Form NC18 — Consent to waive bond

- Form NC20 — Notice to beneficiaries (non-residuary)

- Form NC22 — Notice to spouse of the deceased: *Matrimonial Property Act*

- Form NC23 — Notice to spouse/adult interdependent partner of deceased: *Dependants Relief Act*

- Form NC24.1 — Notice to the Public Trustee

- Form NC25 — Affidavit regarding missing or unknown beneficiaries

We will talk about all of the specialized forms so that you know whether you need each form or not in Chapter 6.

2. Judicial Districts

Alberta is divided into eleven sections called judicial districts, each of which deals with the legal issues that crop up in that geographical area of the province. Your application for probate or administration has to be filed in the judicial district where the deceased person lived (not necessarily where he or she died, as he or she could have been travelling at the time). Check the list below to determine the correct judicial district for your application. If you cannot tell from reading the lists below which is the appropriate judicial district, you may telephone the Clerk of the Court before finalizing your documents to ask whether you have chosen the right district. Telephone numbers for the Clerks of the Court in the different judicial districts are found in Chapter 11, section **5**.

The following are the eleven judicial districts in Alberta, with the names of some of the communities that sit within the borders of the districts (note that this is not a complete list; there are other towns and hamlets within each of these):

- **Calgary:** Airdrie, Balzac, Banff, Bearspaw, Bowden, Bragg Creek, Calgary, Canmore, Carstairs, Cochrane, Cremona, Delacour, Didsbury, Eldon, Exshaw, Gleichen, High River, Horseshoe Lake, Irricana, Kananaskis, Lake Louise, Millarville, Morley, Okotoks, Seebe, Sundre, Turner Valley, Vulcan

- **Drumheller/Hanna:** Baintree, Cambria, Cereal, Dorothy, Drumheller, Dunphy, Halliday, Hanna, Huxley, Kirkpatrick, Kneehill, Oyen, Rainbow, Rockyford, Rosebud, Rosedale, Three Hills, Trochu, Youngstown

- **Edmonton:** Athabasca, Barrhead, Drayton Valley, Edmonton, Edson, Fort Saskatchewan, Fox Creek, Hinton, Jasper, Legal, Mayerthorpe, Morinville, Redwater, Sherwood Park, Spruce Grove, St. Albert, Stony Plain, Swan Hills, Tofield, Vegreville, Viking, Westlock, Whitecourt

- **Fort McMurray:** Anzac, Chard, Conklin, Fort Chipewyan, Fort McKay, Fort McMurray, Fort Smith, Hay River, Janvier, Lynton, Mariana Lake

- **Grande Prairie:** Bear Lake, Beaverlodge, Bluesky, Bredin, Calais, Clairmont, Codesa, Eaglesham, Fox Creek, Grande Prairie, Lassiter, Rycroft, Spirit River, Sturgeon Lake, Teepee Creek, Valleyview, Wembley, Whitemud Creek

- **Lethbridge/Macleod:** Cardston, Fort Macleod, Hillcrest, Kimball, Lethbridge, Magrath, Mekastoe, Milk River, Parkland, Picture Butte, Pincher Creek, Spring Coulee, Stirling, Taber, Travers, Waterton Park, Whiskey Gap

- **Medicine Hat:** Armada, Bassano, Bow Island, Brooks, Duchess, Eagle Butte, Hilda, Illingworth, Medicine Hat, Pinhorn, Redcliff, Roseglen, Sandy Point, Southesk, Thelma, Vale, Woolchester

- **Peace River:** Chinook Valley, Driftpile, Fairview, Falher, Fort Vermilion, Girouxville, Grimshaw, High Level, Peace River, Rainbow Lake, Roma, Slave Lake, Weberville, Worsley, Zama Lake

- **Red Deer:** Caroline, Consort, Coronation, Crimson Lake, Elnora, Erskine, Gleniffer, Innisfail, Joffre, Red Deer, Rocky Mountain House, Stettler, Strachan, Sylvan Lake

- **St. Paul:** Bonnyville, Cold Lake, Elk Point, Lac La Biche, Lloydminster, Saddle Lake, Smoky Lake, St. Paul, Two Hills, Vermilion, Wabasca, Wahstao, Wainwright

- **Wetaskiwin:** Alder Flats, Bashaw, Battle, Beaumont, Buck Lake, Calmar, Camrose, Daysland, Killam, Leduc, Nisku, Ponoka, Sedgewick, Silver Beach, Thorsby, Warburg, Wetaskiwin

3. The Original Will of the Deceased

You must have the original, signed, dated will of the deceased to include in your application for probate. Make several photocopies of the will to save for use later on, but make sure the original will is part of the documentation that goes to the court.

Turn to the very back page of the will (the one where the deceased signed). Flip over that last page. Unless the will is handwritten, it should be stamped and signed by a Commissioner for Oaths, as shown in section **12.** in Chapter 3.

Below that, you will have to add some information. As you will be marking on the back of the original signature page, which is irreplaceable, read this entire section first so that you know what you are doing and take a look at the sample page provided. The purpose of this task is to identify the will as being the one you were talking about when you prepared Form NC4, as well as identifying it as being the one that the witness says he or she saw being signed. This is the way you tell the court that you have attached the right will.

A few inches below the Commissioner's signature, you are going to add the following words and lines. You can type the words or print them neatly, both of which are acceptable, but do not use illegible writing. Add the following:

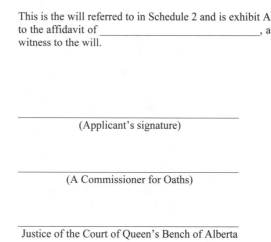

This is the will referred to in Schedule 2 and is exhibit A
to the affidavit of _____, a
witness to the will.

_____
(Applicant's signature)

_____
(A Commissioner for Oaths)

_____
Justice of the Court of Queen's Bench of Alberta

Be sure to leave enough room above the signature lines for people to sign. The line for the judge to sign on should be the last thing on the page. In the blank in the first sentence, fill in the name of the witness who signed the affidavit. Sample 3 is a completed back page for you to use as a reference.

4. Handwritten Wills or Codicils

Handwritten wills and codicils may be sent to the court for probate just as formal documents are, though there are some differences in the procedure. When it comes to typing on the back of the will as set out in the previous section of this chapter, the procedure is the same for handwritten wills as it is for formal wills.

Because handwritten wills do not need witnesses, there may not be anyone who can sign a Form NC8 Affidavit of witness to a will. If that is the case, leave off Form NC8 and do not mark the back of the will as "Exhibit A" as described in section **3.** Instead, complete a Form NC9 Affidavit of handwriting.

5. How to Deal with the Notices

Because the choice of which notices to use is so important, Chapter 12 is devoted to a more detailed description of the notices. That chapter contains step-by-step instructions for completing each notice, so refer to it to decide which notices you need.

Once you have completed the notices you want, print an original of each one. You will see that the executor must sign each and every notice before it is sent out. After the notices are signed, make two photocopies of each of them. You are going to send a copy of each notice out to the

Sample 3
Back of Will

This is Exhibit A to the Affidavit of
_____I.B. Witness_____, sworn before me   *I.M. Witness*
                (name of witness)   *(signature of witness)*
at the City of Lethbridge in the
Province of Alberta, this ___4th___ day
of _____October, 20--_____.

_____
        (signature of commissioner for oaths)
A Commissioner for Oaths in and for the
        Province of Alberta   *(stamp of commissioner for oaths)*

This is the will referred to in Schedule 2 and is exhibit A to the affidavit of
_____I.B. Witness_____, a witness to the will.
        (name of witness [same as witness above])

_____*Lillian France*_____
        (signature of executor)
        (Applicant's signature)

_____
        (signature of commissioner for oaths)
        (A Commissioner for Oaths)

_____
Justice of the Court of Queen's Bench of Alberta

person addressed in the notice using the sample letter provided, but not until your whole Application for Probate is completed. It is important to send the beneficiaries (described in Chapter 12) the photocopy only and to keep the original signed notices. The original notices are going to be put into your Form NC27 Affidavit of service, so you must not mail them to the beneficiaries.

When it is time to send your letters, you will send them by registered mail. Keep the receipts for reimbursement from the estate later.

6. Have Your Documents Commissioned

From time to time, the instructions in this kit will ask you to sign your documents in front of a Commissioner for Oaths. Every document with the word "Affidavit" in its title will need to be signed in front of a Commissioner for Oaths, as the meaning of an affidavit is that it is a sworn document. Any document to be used in an Alberta court that is signed outside of Alberta must be signed in front of a notary public, not a Commissioner for Oaths. This applies to any and all documents, whether signed by the executor or a beneficiary.

If you do not know a Commissioner for Oaths, the following are some ideas for finding one:

- All lawyers and judges are both commissioners and notaries
- Most legal assistants and paralegals are commissioners
- Many real estate offices have commissioners
- Many banks and trust companies have commissioners
- Clerks of the Court (where you file your documents) are commissioners

Many Commissioners for Oaths and notaries public charge a fee for their services. If you have to pay out of your own money for estate documents to be commissioned or notarized, save the receipts so that you can be reimbursed later from estate funds.

7. Now What?

Read Chapter 5 and complete your initial forms for the Grant of Probate application, and read Chapter 6 and complete any specialized documents that apply to your situation.

Once the individual documents that make up your application have been prepared, turn to Chapter 11 to compile your application and file it with the court.

5

Completing the Required Forms for an Application for Probate

All of the forms in this chapter are required on every Application for Probate. Complete these documents first, then look at Chapter 6 to see whether any of the specialized forms apply to your situation.

1. Form NC1 — Application

Form NC1 is a summary of your entire package of documents. It tells the court what the application is about, who is involved, and what you are asking the court to do. Though the title of this document is "Application," once you have completed all of your documents, they together are referred to as your Application for Probate.

Follow these steps to complete your Form NC1:

1. Leave the space for "Court file number" blank as you will not know the number until you file your documents at the court.

2. Fill in the judicial district according to the instructions in Chapter 4, section **2.**

3. Fill in the deceased's full name as shown on the will. It should also match the Certificate of Death or Funeral Director's Statement of Death. If the deceased also had a shortened version of his or her name that appears on any assets, you should include that as well. For example, if Richard Wilson has the name "Rick Wilson"

on his bank account, you will need to include the nickname. You would enter his name as "RICHARD WILSON, A.K.A. RICK WILSON."

4. Under "Bond," you will have to fill in the correct response, which can be determined by reading Chapter 2, section **11.** Delete the responses that do not apply.

5. Under "Notices required," you must list the notices that you will prepare as part of your application. Refer to Chapter 12 to know which notices you need. You do not have to list the names of the people receiving them. Even if there are several people receiving an NC19 Notice to beneficiary (residuary), you only have to list it once. Delete the names of the notices you are not using.

6. Indicate whether or not you are serving a copy of your Application for Probate on the Office of the Public Trustee. Simply fill in "yes" or "no." See Chapter 12, section **11.** if you are not sure whether you should serve them.

7. Fill in your full name as well as the full name of any co-executors who are applying with you. Do not put in the names of alternate executors who are not applying or anyone who has renounced.

8. Under "Complete address for service," fill in one mailing address that can be used by the court or anyone else who needs to send you anything about the application.

9. You will see a signature line on the left hand side of the page and a date line on the right. Sign and date the document. Below the signature line, fill in your full name and your address. If there is more than one executor, you must add a signature line and date line for that executor to use, and fill in the information below the second signature line (i.e., complete address).

10. At the bottom of the page you will see a signature line for the judge and the words "ORDER: ISSUE THE GRANT AS APPLIED FOR." Do not remove or change these words or the signature line.

11. For the Form NC1 document, you should also prepare a backer (see Sample 5). Other documents do not need this. Once the backer is prepared, use it like the back cover of a book. All of your documents with the exception of Form NC27 will be put together as described in Chapter 4, with the backer put on at the end to keep everything together.

Follow these steps to prepare the backer:

1. In the top right hand corner, put in the month and year that you are filing the documents.

2. Leave the court file number blank, as you will not know the number until you file the document at the court.

3. Fill in the same judicial district as you did on Form NC1.

4. Fill in the name of the estate exactly the same as on Form NC1.

5. At the bottom of the document you will see the words "Filed by." Fill in your name (assuming you are the executor) along with your full mailing address, telephone number, and fax number (if you have one).

See Samples 4 and 5 for a filled out example of Form NC1 and a filled out example of a backer. Blank forms are available on the CD-ROM.

2. Form NC2 — Affidavit

An affidavit contains the facts and evidence needed by the court to process the application. The affidavit must be sworn by the executor before a Commissioner for Oaths or Notary Public. If there are co-executors, both must sign and swear the document. Forms NC3 through NC7 are schedules to this affidavit and will be attached to it later.

Follow these steps to complete your Form NC2:

1. Leave the court file number blank until you file your documents at the court.

2. Fill in the same judicial district as you used on your NC1.

3. Fill in the estate name exactly as it appears on the NC1.

4. The deponent is the person who is signing and swearing the NC2 Affidavit. This will always be the person who is going to act as executor. If there is more than one executor, list both names.

5. You will now move to the body, where the paragraphs are numbered.

6. In paragraph 1, you must explain your right to make the application for probate. Choose the words "the personal representative(s) named in the deceased's last will." If you are the second choice of executor named in the Will but the first choice executor has died or renounced, add a brief sentence to explain that. Delete any words in paragraph 1 in the sample form that do not apply to you.

Sample 4
Form NC1

NC1

COURT FILE NUMBER

COURT   **Court of Queen's Bench of Alberta (Surrogate Matter)**

JUDICIAL DISTRICT   Edmonton

ESTATE NAME   Samuel Winston France, a.k.a. Sammy France

PROCEDURE   **Application by the personal representative(s) for a grant of probate**

BOND   **Not required**

NOTICES REQUIRED   **NC19 Notice to beneficiary (residuary)**
NC20 Notice to beneficiary (non-residuary)
NC22 Notice to spouse — Matrimonial Property Act
NC23 Notice to spouse — Dependents Relief Act

COPY OF THE APPLICATION
FILED WITH THE PUBLIC
TRUSTEE'S OFFICE   No
(Yes/No)

PERSONAL
REPRESENTATIVE(S)
NAME(S)   Lillian France

COMPLETE ADDRESS FOR   4500 – 450 Avenue
SERVICE ON THE PERSONAL   Edmonton, Alberta
REPRESENTATIVE(S)   T5T 5T5

_____   November 21, 2011
Personal Representative Name   Date

Complete address: Lillian France
4550 – 450 Avenue
Edmonton, Alberta T5T 5T5

ORDER: ISSUE THE GRANT AS APPLIED FOR

_____   _____
Justice of the Court of Queen's   Date
Bench of Alberta

Sample 5
Document Backer

```
                                                      November 12, 2011
                                                              Date
                                                      Court File No. _____

              IN THE COURT OF QUEEN'S BENCH OF ALBERTA
                         (SURROGATE MATTER)

              JUDICIAL DISTRICT OF _____ Edmonton _____


              The Estate of _____ Samuel Winston France, _____
                    also known as Sammy France, deceased


              APPLICATION FOR PROBATE


                        Filed by: Lillian France
                           4550 – 450 Avenue
                           Edmonton, Alberta
                              T5T 5T5
                        Telephone: 780-123-1234
                           Fax: 780-123-1235
```

7. Under "Schedules attached," list NC3 through NC7 using the number and name of each document. If you are probating a codicil as well as a will, list both NC4 Schedule 2 Will and NC4 Schedule 2 Codicil, as you will be preparing both.

8. You will not make any changes to paragraph 2 unless you are probating a codicil as well as a will. If so, add paragraph 2.6 and list NC4 Schedule 2 Codicil.

9. Under "Documents attached," list the will (e.g., "Will of John James Smith dated January 10, 1998"). Also list the NC8 Affidavit of witness to a will. If you are also probating a codicil, list the codicil as well as the NC8 that goes with it in the same format.

10. You will not make any changes to paragraph 3 unless you are probating a codicil as well as a will. If so, add paragraphs 3.3 for the codicil and 3.4 for the NC8 Affidavit of witness to a codicil.

11. In paragraph 4 you must list the notices you are going to serve and delete the notices you are not going to serve. You do not need to include the names of the people who will be served. This list should match the list you made in the NC1 application.

12. Do not change paragraphs 5 or 6.

13. Fill in the place and date that the NC2 Affidavit is being signed and sworn.

14. You will see a signature line with the word "deponent" below it. Remove the word "deponent" and put in your name. If there is more than one executor, make a new signature line and put in that person's name. You do not need to put in a new signature line for the Commissioner for Oaths if both executors swear the document at the same time.

See Sample 6 for a filled-out example. A blank form is available on the CD-ROM.

3. Form NC3 — Schedule 1: Deceased

The purpose of Form NC3 is to give the court a full description of the deceased person and his or her family members.

Follow these steps to complete your Form NC3:

1. At the top of the page beside "Estate name," add the name of the deceased exactly as it appears on your NC1 application.

2. Under "Name," fill in the deceased's name as it appears on the will.

3. In the following line, fill in any other names, such as maiden name, other married names, or nicknames.

4. For the residence address, fill in the full street address and mailing address, including postal code. If the deceased passed away in a hospital or other facility but had a home that he or she usually lived in when not ill, fill in the address of the usual home, not the facility.

5. Fill in the deceased's exact date of birth.

6. Fill in the deceased's place of birth by naming the town/city and the province, state or country. No street address is required.

7. Fill in the deceased's exact date of death.

8. Fill in the deceased's place of death. This does not refer to a hospital, care facility, or mailing address. It only requires the town/city and province, state or country. If the deceased died away from home on a vacation or business trip, fill in the name of the city or town he or she was in when he or she died.

Sample 6
Form NC2

NC2

COURT FILE NUMBER

COURT   **Court of Queen's Bench of Alberta (Surrogate Matter)**

JUDICIAL DISTRICT   Edmonton

ESTATE NAME   Samuel Winston France, a.k.a. Sammy France

DOCUMENT   **Affidavit by the personal representative(s) on application for a grant of probate**

DEPONENT(S) NAME(S)   Lillian France

THE DEPONENT(S) EACH SWEAR UNDER OATH OR AFFIRM THAT THE INFORMATION IN THIS AFFIDAVIT AND IN THE ATTACHED SCHEDULES IS WITHIN THE DEPONENTS' KNOWLEDGE AND IS TRUE. WHERE THE INFORMATION IS BASED ON ADVICE OR INFORMATION AND BELIEF, THIS IS STATED.

Applicant(s):

1. The applicant is entitled to apply for a grant because the applicant is named as the personal representative in the deceased's last Will.

Schedules Attached:

2. The following schedules are part of this affidavit. They are correct to the deponents' information and belief.

    2.1   NC3 Schedule 1 Deceased
    2.2   NC4 Schedule 2 Will
    2.3   NC5 Schedule 3 Personal representative(s)
    2.4   NC6 Schedule 4 Beneficiaries
    2.5   NC7 Schedule 5 Inventory

Documents Attached:

3. The following documents are part of this affidavit.

    3.1   Original will of the deceased
    3.2   NC8 Affidavit of witness to a will

    The schedules and documents that are part of this affidavit provide all the information required in this application by the Surrogate Rules and have been prepared by me.

Sample 6 — Continued

Notices:

4. The applicant(s) will serve the following notices as required and in the manner prescribed by the Surrogate Rules.

   4.1   NC19 Notice(s) to beneficiaries (residuary)
   4.2   NC20 Notice(s) to beneficiaries (non residuary)
   4.3   NC22 Notice to spouse of deceased *Matrimonial Property Act*

   (Include the following if applicable. Delete if not applicable.)

5. The applicant(s) will not make a distribution to a trustee of any property that is subject to a trust under the will until after an acknowledgment of trustee(s) in Form NC6.1 signed by the trustee(s) has been filed.

6. The applicant(s) will faithfully administer the estate of the deceased according to law and will give a true accounting of their administration to the persons entitled to it when lawfully required.

SWORN OR AFFIRMED BY EACH DEPONENT BEFORE A COMMISSIONER FOR
OATHS AT _____Edmonton_____, ALBERTA ON _____November 21, 2011_____.

_____Lillian France_____   _____
        Deponent   Commissioner's Name

                                               _____
                                               Appointment Expiry Date

9. Fill in the province or state that the deceased usually lived in. This should in most cases be Alberta. If this is not your answer, consider whether you are applying in the right jurisdiction for your probate.

10. Next, you will give information to the court about the members of the deceased's immediate family. Leave in the sentence about immediate family members being over 18 and not disabled. This puts the responsibility on you to point out any family members who are not over 18, or who are physically or mentally disabled.

11. Under the heading of "SPOUSE," fill in the spouse's full name and complete street and mailing address if the deceased was legally married (NOT common law). If there is no legally married spouse, state "none."

12. Under the heading of "ADULT INTERDEPENDENT PARTNER," if the deceased lived in a common-law relationship, either opposite-sex or same-sex, fill in the partner's full name and complete street and mailing address. If there was no common-law partner, state "none" and delete the rest of the paragraphs under the ADULT INTERDEPENDENT PARTNER heading.

13. If you fill in a name under ADULT INTERDEPENDENT PARTNER, you must select one of the next three paragraphs to include in the document. The two you do not select may be deleted. Fill in one of the following:

   • In the paragraph that begins with "for a continuous period of not less than 3 years," fill in the date that the deceased began living with his/her partner, and the date that they stopped living together. If they were still living together when the deceased died, you may say "on the death of the deceased" for the ending date;

   • In the paragraph that begins with "of some permanence of which there is a child," fill in the date that the deceased's child with his/her partner was born or adopted;

   • In the paragraph that begins with "The adult interdependent partner entered into an agreement," fill in the date that the agreement was signed.

14. Check off whether the person named as the common-law partner (adult interdependent partner) is related to the deceased by blood or adoption.

15. Under the heading of "CHILDREN," you will see five lines of information starting with "Name" and ending with "Died leaving children." For each child of the deceased, regardless of age, you must supply all of this information. Cut and paste the questions as many times as you need to. If there are no children, simply state "none."

16. If a child of the deceased is 18 or older, under "age" you may simply put "over 18." The purpose of this question is to identify minors.

17. If a child is a minor, fill in the exact birthday next to "date of birth." You do not need to include birth dates for anyone who is 18 or older.

18. If a child of the deceased has died before the deceased, fill in the date that the child died.

19. If a child of the deceased has died before the deceased, fill in either "yes" or "no" to the question of whether that child died leaving children of his/her own (i.e., grandchildren of the deceased).

20. If no child of the deceased has passed away, you may remove the lines referring to the death of a child.

21. Under "FORMER SPOUSES," you only need to include:
    - any spouse to whom the deceased was legally married (not common law) and who was divorced from the deceased within the two years prior to the deceased's death, OR
    - any spouse (legally married, not common law) who has been divorced from the deceased for more than two years, but the division of property or assets has not been finalized.

22. If there is no such spouse, you may simply say "none." If the family situation is complicated (for example with several children with different surnames), including the names of former spouses can be helpful to the court to figure out who is who.

See Sample 7 for a filled-out example. A blank form is available on the CD-ROM.

4. Form NC4 — Schedule 2: Will

The purpose of Form NC4 is to summarize the information about the will that is being probated. All of the information you will need is included in the will itself. If you are also probating a codicil, complete another NC4 for the codicil. You will complete an NC4 even if the will you are probating is a handwritten will.

Follow these steps to complete your Form NC4:

1. Fill in the estate name exactly as it appears on your NC1 application.

2. Fill in the deceased's age on the day he or she signed the will. If the deceased was not yet 18 years old when he or she signed, you must explain why he or she was able to make a valid will while still a minor. Your choices are:

   • The deceased was married.

   • The deceased had an adult interdependent partner.

   • The deceased had a child.

   • The deceased was in the Canadian Forces and was on active service.

   • The deceased was a mariner or seaman.

3. Under "Marriages," you need only mention marriages that occurred after the will was signed. If there was no such marriage, say "none" and remove all other words in this section. If the deceased did marry after the will was signed, fill in the full name of the spouse and the date of the marriage. You will note that you are also including the words "as contemplated in the will." Check the will to make sure that it contains a clause about being made in contemplation of marriage. If it does not, the will is void and cannot be probated.

4. Fill in the name of the two witnesses to the will. If the will was handwritten and did not have witnesses, add the words "the will was handwritten and did not have witnesses."

5. Leave in the sentence that neither witness was a beneficiary or the spouse of a beneficiary. Check the will to make sure that is true. If not, the will is still valid but the gift to the witness/ beneficiary is not.

6. The last line to be filled in is asking about anything that was handwritten into the will or crossed out. If nothing was changed

Sample 7
Form NC3

NC3

ESTATE NAME   Samuel Winston France, a.k.a. Sammy France

DOCUMENT   **Schedule 1: Deceased**

Name: Samuel Winston France
Any other name(s) by which known: Sammy France
Last residence address in full: 122 Apple Boulevard, Edmonton, Alberta, T5T 4T4
Date of birth: February 22, 1936
Place of birth: Calgary, Alberta
Date of death: October 1, 2011
Place of death: Leduc, Alberta
Habitual province/state of residence: Alberta
The deceased died Testate.

IMMEDIATE FAMILY

All immediate family members are over 18 and physically and mentally competent unless otherwise shown.

[   ] SPOUSE
       Name (or state none, if applicable): <u>None</u>
       Complete address: _____

[   ] ADULT INTERDEPENDENT PARTNER
       Name (or state none, if applicable): <u>None</u>
       Complete address: _____

       [   ] the adult interdependent partner lived with the deceased in a relationship of
           interdependence
       [   ] for a continuous period of not less than 3 years commencing
           _____ and ending _____.
       [   ] of some permanence of which there is a child

           [   ] born _____
                              date
           [   ] adopted _____
                                date

       [   ] the adult interdependent partner entered into an adult interdependent partner
           agreement with the deceased which agreement is dated _____.

       The adult interdependent partner

           [   ] is
           [   ] is not

       related to the deceased by blood or adoption.

[X] CHILDREN
Except as otherwise provided, all of the deceased's children are over 18 years of age at the time of the deceased's death, and none is unable by reason of mental or physical disability to earn a livelihood.
Name (or state none, if applicable): Lillian France
Complete address: 4550 – 450 Avenue, Edmonton, Alberta, T5T 5T5
Age: over 18   Date of birth:
Date of death:
Died leaving children:

[X] FORMER SPOUSES (Who require notice under the *Matrimonial Property Act*)
Name (or state none, if applicable): Mirabelle France
Complete address: 555 Green Street, Airdrie, Alberta, T5T 4T4
Date of death:
Date of divorce: June 15, 2011

or added, fill in the words "there appear to be no erasures, changes, or other additions to the will." If there are handwritten changes, state what they are as briefly and clearly as you can. For example: "On the bottom of the last page of the will, the word June was crossed out and the word July was handwritten in right above it."

7. Print your document and attach it to the NC2 Affidavit.

See Sample 8 for a filled out example. A blank form is available on the CD-ROM.

5.   Form NC5 — Schedule 3: Personal Representative(s)

The purpose of Form NC5 is to give the court information about you and to establish your right to be the one to apply for probate. Remember that the phrase "personal representative" includes executors and administrators. If there are two executors, do not make a separate NC5, just simply add one person's information below the other.

Sample 8
Form NC4

NC4

ESTATE NAME   Samuel Winston France, a.k.a. Sammy France

DOCUMENT   **Schedule 2: Will**

Date of will: August 12, 1991

Deceased's age at date of will: 56

Marriages of deceased subsequent to date of will: None

Adult interdependent partner agreements entered into by deceased subsequent to date of will: None

Name of first witness: Charlene Hightower

Name of second witness: Jim Middlemarch

Neither witness is a beneficiary or the spouse or adult interdependent partner of a beneficiary named in the will.

To the best of the personal representative(s) information and belief, this is the deceased's original last will.

The personal representative(s) have examined the will and observe that
no handwritten changes were made to it .

Follow these steps to complete your Form NC5:

1. Fill in the estate name exactly as it is shown on your NC1 application.

2. Fill in the full legal name of the executor(s).

3. Fill in the complete mailing addresses of the executor(s) including postal code.

4. Under "Status," you must indicate why you are the right person to apply for probate. In almost every case, you will choose "Named in the will" as your reason for applying.

5. Fill in your relationship to the deceased (e.g. spouse, sibling, friend).

6. Do not change the sentence regarding age, as you must be 18 years or older to apply to be an executor.

7. If there is anyone with a greater or equal right to apply, you must fill in his or her name and relationship in the next line. The only

circumstances in which there would be someone with that kind of right are —

- you are the alternate executor named and the first-named executor is not applying for any reason, or

- you are a co-executor and the other co-executor is not applying with you.

8. If either of the circumstances described above fits your situation, then somebody has likely renounced. If so, list their names here and attach their written, signed Renunciations to the NC2 affidavit.

9. Attach your completed Form NC5 to the Form NC2 Affidavit.

See Sample 9 for a filled out example. A blank form is available on the CD-ROM.

6. Form NC6 — Schedule 4: Beneficiaries

The Form NC6 is used to describe to the court who is going to get what under the will (and codicil, if applicable). You will have to read the will, then figure out how it applies to the individual people in the deceased's life.

Follow these steps to complete your Form NC6:

1. Fill in the estate name exactly as it was shown on your Form NC1 application.

2. The six items to fill in — starting with "Name" and proceeding down to "Para. no will" must be repeated for each and every beneficiary of the estate. Depending on the gifts set out in the will, this could make your NC6 very lengthy, but that is perfectly alright. You may cut and paste the six items before filling in any information.

3. Under "Name," fill in the full legal name of the beneficiary (not nicknames).

4. Fill in the relationship of the beneficiary to the deceased (e.g., child, sibling, friend). If the beneficiary is a charity, fill in "none."

5. Fill in the complete mailing address and street address of the beneficiary.

6. Under "Age," you need only put in a specific age if the beneficiary was not yet 18 years old on the day the deceased died. If

Sample 9
Form NC5

NC5

ESTATE NAME   Samuel Winston France, a.k.a. Sammy France
DOCUMENT   **Schedule 3: Personal representative(s)**

Name(s): Lillian France

Complete address(es): 4550 – 450 Avenue, Edmonton, Alberta, T5T 5T5

Status: Named in the deceased's Will

Relationship to deceased: Daughter

Age: over 18

Any persons with a prior or
equal right to apply: No

Renunciations attached: No

the beneficiary was 18 years old or older on the day the deceased died, fill in "over 18."

7. Under "Nature of gift" you should very briefly describe what the beneficiary is going to receive under the will. It is best to follow the wording of the will as closely as possible.

8. Fill in the paragraph number of the will that gives the beneficiary the gift.

9. Remember to repeat all of the above information for each beneficiary.

10. The last question on this form asks you to list any gifts that are void because the will was improperly witnessed. If there are no gifts to list, simply state "none." If the will was witnessed by a beneficiary, or the spouse or common-law spouse of a beneficiary, any and all gifts to that beneficiary must be listed here as being void.

See Sample 10 for a filled out example. A blank form is available on the CD-ROM.

Sample 10
Form NC6

NC6

ESTATE NAME   Samuel Winston France, a.k.a. Sammy France

DOCUMENT   **Schedule 4: Beneficiaries**

Name(s): Lillian France

Relationship: Daughter

Complete address: 4550 – 450 Avenue, Edmonton, Alberta, T5T 5T5

Age: over 18

Nature of gift: 100% of estate

Para. no. will: 3 (10)

Except as otherwise provided, all beneficiaries are mentally capable.

The following gifts are void because the beneficiary is a witness or the spouse or adult interdependent partner of a witness to the will:

7. Form NC7 — Schedule 5: Inventory of Property and Debts

Because Form NC7 is the most complicated and the most time-consuming of all of the forms, there is a separate chapter in this kit devoted to preparing it (see Chapter 7).

See Sample 17 in Chapter 7 for a filled out example. A blank form is available on the CD-ROM.

8. Form NC8 — Affidavit of Witness to a Will

The purpose of the Form NC8 is to give the court evidence that all of the rules that apply to the signing of wills were followed when the will was signed. If you are probating a will and a codicil together, you will need one Form NC8 for the will and a second Form NC8 for the codicil. If the will and/or codicil were prepared by a lawyer, it is likely that the Form NC8 is already prepared.

Follow these steps to complete your Form NC8:

1. Fill in the testator's name (i.e. the name of the deceased) exactly as it appears on the will. This should match the name you have been using on your forms.

2. The deponent is the person who witnessed the will being signed and who is going to swear the affidavit. Fill in this person's name in full.

3. Fill in the date that the affidavit is being sworn.

4. Under "Exhibit attached," fill in the date that the will was signed by the deceased. If for a codicil, change the word "will" to "codicil."

5. Do not change the sentences that appear in all capital letters.

6. In paragraph 1, fill in the deceased's name exactly as you did at the top of the page.

7. In paragraph 2, fill in the date the will was signed.

8. Do not change paragraph 3.

9. In paragraph 5, fill in the name of the second witness.

10. In paragraph 6, describe any handwritten changes or anything crossed out. Only include changes that were initialed by the testator AND the two witnesses, so that it is clear that the changes were made before the will was signed.

11. On the back of the original will, type the following exactly as it is shown here:

> This is Exhibit A to the Affidavit of
> _____, sworn before me
> at the City of _____, in the
>
> _____
> Province of Alberta, this _____ day
> of _____.
>
>
> _____
> A Commissioner for Oaths in and for the
> Province of Alberta

12. The witness (also known as the deponent) must now take the Form NC8 along with the original will to a Commissioner for Oaths to sign and swear it.

13. The Commissioner for Oaths will sign, date, and stamp the Form NC8 and the original will and give it back to you.

See Sample 11 for a filled out example of Form NC8. A blank form is available on the CD-ROM.

9. Form NC19 — Notice to Beneficiaries (Residuary)

In Form NC19, you are letting each residuary beneficiary of the estate know about his or her entitlement under the estate. To determine which beneficiaries are the residuary beneficiaries, look for language such as "I leave the residue of my estate to ... " or "I divide the rest of my estate equally among ... " A homemade will might simply say "I leave my estate to ... " Each beneficiary gets a separate notice, even if there is more than one beneficiary at the same address.

For instructions on completing Form NC19, see Chapter 12. A blank form is available on the CD-ROM.

10. Form NC27 — Affidavit of Service

The purpose of the NC27 is to give evidence that you served the right notices on the right people as part of your application. Because this document is an affidavit, it must be sworn before a Commissioner for Oaths.

Chapter 12 gives step-by-step directions for completing Form NC27. Once you have completed it, attached your exhibits, signed it, and sworn it in front of a Commissioner for Oaths, you will submit it to the court at the same time as your Application for Probate. In fact, the Clerk of the Court likely will not allow you to file your Application for Probate unless it is accompanied by the NC27 Affidavit of service.

See Chapter 12 for a filled out example of Form NC27. A blank form is available on the CD-ROM.

To ensure you have all of the documents you need for your application, see Checklist 3.

Sample 11
Form NC8

NC8

TESTATOR NAME	Samuel Winston France, a.k.a. Sammy France
DOCUMENT	**Affidavit of witness to a will**
DEPONENT'S NAME	Charlene Hightower
EXHIBIT ATTACHED	**A: Original will dated** August 12, 1991

THE DEPONENT SWEARS UNDER OATH OR AFFIRMS THAT THE
INFORMATION IN THIS AFFIDAVIT IS WITHIN THE DEPONENT'S
KNOWLEDGE AND IS TRUE. WHERE THE INFORMATION IS BASED ON
ADVICE OR INFORMATION AND BELIEF, THIS IS STATED.

1. I am one of the subscribing witnesses to the last will of the deceased, Samuel Winston France .

2. The will is dated August 12, 1991 and is marked as Exhibit A to this affidavit.

3. When the deceased signed the will, I believe the deceased understood that the document being signed was the deceased's will.

4. When the deceased signed the will, I believe the deceased was competent to sign the will.

5. The deceased, myself and the other witness to the will, Jim Middlemarch , were all present together when the witnesses and the deceased signed the will.

6. Before the deceased signed the will, the deceased made the following changes to it:
   6.1 None .

SWORN OR AFFIRMED BEFORE A COMMISSIONER FOR OATHS AT
Edmonton , ALBERTA ON November 21, 2011 .

Charlene Hightower
Deponent

_____
Commissioner's Name

_____
Appointment Expiry Date

Checklist 3
Documents Required on Every Application for Probate

Document	Done	Notes
Original will		
Form NC1 — Application by the personal representative for a grant of probate		
Form NC2 — Affidavit by the personal representative(s) on application for a grant of probate		
Form NC3 — Schedule 1: Deceased		
Form NC4 — Schedule 2: Will		
Form NC5 — Schedule 3: Personal representatives		
Form NC6 — Schedule 4: Beneficiaries		
Form NC7 — Schedule 5: Inventory		
Form NC8 — Affidavit of witness to will (mark the back of the original will as Exhibit A to this affidavit)		
Form NC19 — Notice to beneficiaries (residuary)		
Form NC27 — Affidavit of service		

6

Completing the Specialized Forms for an Application for Probate

In this chapter, you will find the descriptions of a number of documents that are not always needed in applications, but which may be needed in your case. Each document is described individually, with clear instructions so you can decide whether or not you need to complete that document. Make sure you only use the documents you need.

You will notice as you prepare your documents that Form NC11 is used more than once. This is because Form NC11 is designed to give evidence that a document was signed a certain way and is used with several different forms. In this kit, we have attached a Form NC11 to each document that requires it on the CD-ROM, and it will be slightly different each time you prepare it. This form is currently only required where it has been provided.

1. Form NC9 — Affidavit of Handwriting of Deceased

Use Form NC9 only if the will or codicil you are probating is handwritten and not typed or computer generated. If the will is partly handwritten and partly typed, such as a form from a kit, do not use Form NC9. Go back to the previous chapter and use Form NC8 instead.

Follow these steps to complete your Form NC9:

1. Fill in the estate name exactly as you did on Form NC1.

2. The deponent is the person who is going to give evidence about the deceased's handwriting and swear the evidence to be true. Fill in the deponent's name in the second line.

3. Fill in the date that the deceased signed his/her will.

4. Do not change the sentence that appears in all capital letters.

5. In paragraph 1, fill in the deceased's name as it appears at the top of this form and put in the number of years that the deponent knew him or her.

6. If there is more information that the deponent would like to add, such as describing how it came about that he or she saw the deceased's handwriting, fill in as many numbered paragraphs as is necessary. Examples of the person's contact with his or her handwriting might be that they corresponded by mail for several years, or that he or she was his accountant and he brought his handwritten notes to him or her. Whatever can be thought of that is persuasive can be added here.

7. After you have added any additional lines, put in the paragraph that is marked number 2 on the sample. Fill in the date of the will.

8. The deponent will have to pick one of the two choices for paragraph 3. Note that the first choice refers to a will where the whole thing is in handwriting. The second choice refers to a will that is fully or partially typewritten, on a form, or written by someone else, and is signed by the deceased. Delete the sentence that isn't used, and fill in the page number if the second option is chosen.

9. Fill in the date that the affidavit is signed and sworn.

10. The deponent must sign and swear Form NC9 in front of a Commissioner for Oaths. He or she must have the original will with him/her because it is going to be marked as exhibit A.

See Sample 12 for Form NC9.

2. Form NC12 — Renunciation of Probate

Use Form NC12 only if the executor named in the will has chosen not to be the executor and the alternate named is going to act as executor instead, or if one of the named co-executors has decided not to act.

Sample 12
Form NC9

NC9

ESTATE NAME	Samuel Winston France, a.k.a. Sammy France
DOCUMENT	**Affidavit of handwriting of deceased**
DEPONENT'S NAME	Bill Smith
EXHIBIT ATTACHED	**A: Will dated**

THE DEPONENT SWEARS UNDER OATH OR AFFIRMS THAT THE INFORMATION IN THIS AFFIDAVIT IS WITHIN THE DEPONENT'S KNOWLEDGE AND IS TRUE. WHERE THE INFORMATION IS BASED ON ADVICE OR INFORMATION AND BELIEF, THIS IS STATED.

1. I knew the deceased, ___Samuel Winston France___, well and for ___twenty___ years before the deceased died. I frequently saw the deceased write and sign documents and I am very familiar with the deceased's handwriting and signature.

2. I have carefully examined the document dated ___August 12, 1991___ which purports to be the deceased's last will and which is marked as Exhibit A to this affidavit.

3. I believe that the signature appearing on page __4__ of the Will is that of the deceased.

SWORN OR AFFIRMED BEFORE A COMMISSIONER FOR OATHS AT
_____Edmonton_____, ALBERTA ON _____November 21, 2011_____.

_____*Bill Smith*_____   _____
Deponent   Commissioner's Name

                                  _____
                                  Appointment Expiry Date

Follow these steps to fill in your Form NC12:

1. Fill in the estate name exactly as you did on Form NC1.

2. Fill in the name and complete address including postal code of the person who is going to renounce.

3. In paragraph 1, fill in the name of the deceased exactly as it is seen on the will.

4. Do not change paragraphs 2 and 3.

5. Fill in the date that the person signed it.

6. The person renouncing must sign on the signature line on the left hand side of the page in front of a witness.

7. The witness must sign above the signature line on the right hand side of the page.

Form NC12 has a second page. It is titled NC11, but must be stapled to and kept with Form NC12. The second page is proof that Form NC12 was properly signed. The NC11 must be signed and sworn by the witness in front of a Commissioner for Oaths.

1. At the top of Form NC11, fill in the estate name exactly as you did on Form NC1.

2. The deponent is the same person as the witness who signed on the right hand side of Form NC12. Fill in the name of the deponent.

3. Fill in the date that the deponent signs.

4. Do not change the sentence that appears in all capital letters.

5. In paragraph 1, fill in the name of the person who signed Form NC12 (not the witness).

6. In paragraph 2, fill in the same name again, then fill in the name of the city, town, or hamlet in Alberta where Form NC12 was signed (this may be different from where Form NC11 is signed).

7. You will have to choose between two forms of paragraph 3. Use the first one if the person who signed Form NC12 is someone that the witness/deponent knows personally. Use the second one if the person who signed Form NC12 is someone that the witness/deponent does not know personally but who he or she can identify by looking at his/her identification. Delete the version of paragraph 3 that you do not use.

8. In paragraph 4, fill in the name of the person who signed Form NC12.

9. The Commissioner for Oaths will fill in the place and date that the Form NC11 is signed.

10. The deponent/witness must sign on the signature line on the left hand side of Form NC11 only when he or she is in front of the Commissioner for Oaths.

11. The Commissioner for Oaths will sign, date and stamp the document on the right hand side of the page.

See Sample 13 for a sample of Form NC12.

3. Form NC17 — Affidavit to Dispense with a Bond

Use NC17 if:

- you are the only executor and you live outside of Alberta;

- there is more than one executor, but none live in Alberta;

- you believe that a bond is not necessary to ensure that the executor's work will be completed honestly and properly;

- you do not wish to post a bond;

- you have chosen "request to waive" on your Form NC1; and

- you are also filing a Form NC18.

Follow these steps to fill in your Form NC17:

1. Fill in the estate name exactly as you did on the NC1.

2. Fill in the name of the person who will be swearing the affidavit (i.e., the deponent). This should be the executor.

3. Fill in the date that the affidavit is sworn before a Commissioner for Oaths.

4. Do not change the sentence that appears in all capital letters.

5. In paragraph 2, describe how you are related to the deceased. If you are not related by blood, describe whether you are a friend, pastor, brother-in-law, caregiver, employee, etc.

6. Do not change paragraphs 3 and 4. If you cannot swear under oath that both of those paragraphs are true, do not complete the NC17.

Sample 13
Form NC12

NC12

ESTATE NAME	Samuel Winston France, a.k.a. Sammy France
DOCUMENT	**Renunciation of probate**
NAME	Jill Smith
COMPLETE ADDRESS	123 Main Street, Edmonton, Alberta, T5T 1H1

1. The deceased, ___Samuel Winston France___, signed a will in which I am appointed personal representative.

2. I renounce all my right and title to a grant of probate of the deceased's will.

3. I have not intermeddled in the deceased's estate.

SIGNED ON _____December 10, 2011_____ .

Jill Smith
Signature

Bill McDonald
Witness

This document must have Form NC11 attached.

NC11

ESTATE NAME   Samuel Winston France, a.k.a. Sammy France

DOCUMENT   **Affidavit of Witness to Signature on Renunciation of Probate**

DEPONENT'S NAME   Bill McDonald

THE DEPONENT SWEARS UNDER OATH OR AFFIRMS THAT THE INFORMATION IN THIS AFFIDAVIT IS WITHIN THE DEPONENT'S KNOWLEDGE AND IS TRUE. WHERE THE INFORMATION IS BASED ON ADVICE OR INFORMATION AND BELIEF, THIS IS STATED.

1. I am the witness to the signature of _____Jill Smith_____ in this Renunciation of Probate.

2. I was present and saw _____Jill Smith_____ sign this document at _____Edmonton_____, Alberta.

3. I know _____Jill Smith_____ to be the person named in this Renunciation of Probate.

4. I believe that _____Jill Smith_____ is at least 18 years of age.

SWORN OR AFFIRMED BEFORE A COMMISSIONER FOR OATHS AT _____Edmonton_____, ALBERTA ON _____December 10, 2011_____.

_____*Bill McDonald*_____
Deponent

_____
Commissioner's Name

_____
Appointment Expiry Date

Sample 14
Form NC17

NC17

ESTATE NAME	Samuel Winston France, a.k.a. Sammy France
DOCUMENT	**Affidavit to dispense with a bond**
DEPONENT'S NAME	Lillian France

THE DEPONENT SWEARS UNDER OATH OR AFFIRMS THAT THE
INFORMATION IN THIS AFFIDAVIT IS WITHIN THE DEPONENT'S
KNOWLEDGE AND IS TRUE. WHERE THE INFORMATION IS BASED
ON ADVICE OR INFORMATION AND BELIEF, THIS IS STATED.

Applicant

1. The applicant is entitled to apply for a grant because the applicant is
    _____his daughter_____.

2. The applicant is fully familiar with the deceased's affairs because she is related to the
    deceased as _____his daughter_____.

Debts

3. The applicant has made a complete investigation of the deceased's affairs. To the best
    of my knowledge, Schedule 5 shows all the debts for which the deceased may be
    liable in the Province of Alberta and in any other jurisdiction.

4. The property of the estate is sufficient to pay all the debts shown in Schedule 5 and
    all the debts have been or will be paid before the distribution of the estate.

Special matters

5. _____
    _____

6. And therefore the applicant requests that this Court grant the application for a grant of
    probate without bond.

SWORN OR AFFIRMED BY THE DEPONENT BEFORE A COMMISSIONER FOR
OATHS AT _____Edmonton_____, ALBERTA ON _____December 10, 2011_____.

_____   _____
          Deponent   Commissioner's Name

                                          _____
                                            Appointment Expiry Date

7. Fill in the name of the town or city where the document was signed and sworn. If there is more than one executor, repeat the jurat (the line that shows in all capitals) and the signature line.

See Sample 14 for a sample of Form NC17.

4. Form NC18 — Consent to Waive Bond

Form NC18 is not signed by the executor; it is signed by the residuary beneficiaries of the estate. Each beneficiary must have his or her own Form NC18 to sign. You should prepare the documents for them, and once signed, the forms should be returned to you.

The purpose of the document is to tell the court that the beneficiaries of the estate are aware the executor is applying to dispense with the bond, and they feel secure in allowing the executor to go ahead without it.

The document does not have to be sworn in front of a Commissioner for Oaths, but it does need to have a witness watch the beneficiary sign. The executor should not be the witness on this form, though the beneficiaries can be witnesses for each other.

Follow these steps to fill in your Form NC18:

1. Fill in the estate name exactly as you did on Form NC1.

2. Fill in the name of the beneficiary as it appears in the will.

3. Fill in the beneficiary's full address, including postal code.

4. In paragraph 1, fill in the name of the deceased.

5. In paragraph 2, fill in the name of the executor(s).

6. Fill in the date the document was signed by the beneficiary.

7. Have the beneficiary sign on the line on the left hand side of the form.

8. Have a witness sign on the right hand side of the form.

9. The witness should clearly print his or her name below the signature.

Form NC18 has a second page. The second page is titled NC11, but must be stapled to and kept with the page titled NC18. The second page is the proof that Form NC18 was properly signed. Form NC11 must be signed and sworn by the witness in front of a Commissioner for Oaths.

1. At the top of Form NC11, fill in the estate name exactly as you did on Form NC1.

2. The deponent is the same person as the witness who signed Form NC18. Fill in the name of the deponent.

3. Fill in the date that the deponent signs.

4. Do not change the sentence that appears in all capital letters.

5. In paragraph 1, fill in the name of the person who signed Form NC18 (not the witness).

6. In paragraph 2, fill in the same name again, then fill in the name of the city, town, or hamlet in Alberta where Form NC18 was signed (this may be different from where Form NC11 is signed).

7. You will have to choose between two forms of paragraph 3. Use the first one if the person signing Form NC18 is someone the witness/deponent knows personally. Use the second one if the person signing Form NC18 is someone the witness/deponent does not know personally but who he or she can identify by looking at his/her identification. Delete the version of paragraph 3 that you do not use.

8. In paragraph 4, fill in the name of the person who signed Form NC18.

9. The Commissioner for Oaths will fill in the place and date the Form NC11 is signed.

10. The deponent/witness must sign on the signature line on the left hand side of Form NC11 only when he or she is in front of the Commissioner for Oaths.

11. The Commissioner for Oaths will sign, date, and stamp the document on the right hand side of the page.

See Sample 15 for an example of Form NC18.

5. Form NC20 — Notice to Beneficiaries (Non Residuary)

Use Form NC20 if there is at least one person who is receiving a specific item (e.g., a ring, a vehicle) or specific sum of money (e.g., a gift of cash to a charity). This covers every beneficiary who is not receiving part of the residue. You will prepare a separate notice for each beneficiary. If a beneficiary is receiving a specific item as well as part of the residue, you should prepare both a Form NC20 and a Form NC19 for that person.

To fill in a Form NC20, see Chapter 12.

Sample 15
Form NC18

NC18

ESTATE NAME	Samuel Winston France, a.k.a. Sammy France
DOCUMENT	**Consent to waive bond**
NAME	Benjamin France
COMPLETE ADDRESS	1211 S. Sierra Boulevard, Edmonton, Alberta, T1H 1H1

1. The deceased, ___Samuel Winston France___, died testate.

2. _____Lillian France_____, who resides outside Alberta, is appointed personal representative in the deceased's will and is applying for a grant of probate.

3. I have an interest in the administration of the deceased's estate because I am _____a beneficiary_____.

4. I understand that a bond is required because the applicant(s) reside outside Alberta. Nevertheless, I consent to an order of the court dispensing with any bond so required.

SIGNED ON _____December 15, 2011_____.

_____B. France_____
Signature

_____I.M. Witness_____
Witness

This document must have Form NC11 attached.

6. Form NC22 — Notice to Spouse of Deceased: *Matrimonial Property Act*

Use Form NC22 if —

- the deceased was legally married (not common law) when he or she died; and

- the will does not leave 100 percent of the estate to the spouse.

Also use Form NC22 if —

- the deceased was legally married (not common law) when he or she died; and

- there is no will.

To fill in Form NC22, see Chapter 12.

7. Form NC23 — Notice to Spouse/Adult Interdependent Partner of Deceased: *Dependants Relief Act*

Use NC23 if —

- the deceased was legally married or had an adult interdependent partner at the time he or she died (see Chapter 12 for an explanation of adult interdependent partner);

- the spouse or adult interdependent partner resided in Canada at the time the deceased died; and

- the will does not leave 100 percent of the estate to the spouse or adult interdependent partner.

Also use NC23 if —

- the deceased was legally married or had an adult interdependent partner at the time he or she died;

- the spouse or adult interdependent partner resided in Canada at the time the deceased died; and

- there is no will.

To fill in Form NC23, see Chapter 12.

8. Form NC24.1 — Notice to the Public Trustee

Use NC24.1 if —

- there is a beneficiary of the estate who is not yet 18 years old;

- there is a beneficiary of the estate who is 18 or older now but was not yet 18 on the day the deceased died;

- the deceased left a biological or adopted child who is under the age of 18, even if the child is not named in the will;

- a beneficiary is missing (i.e., you know who it is but his or her whereabouts are unknown);

- the Public Trustee is the court-appointed trustee for a beneficiary of the estate; or

- the Public Trustee is the attorney under an Enduring Power of Attorney for a beneficiary of the estate.

To fill in your Form NC24.1, see Chapter 12.

9. Form NC25 — Affidavit Regarding Missing or Unknown Beneficiaries

Not many estates require this form. It is intended to be used where there is difficulty identifying or finding a beneficiary and the entire estate is being delayed while the executor searches for the person. Normally, the executor would keep searching and making enquiries, but if the executor has determined that the searches are pointless for now and the estate would be better off if the executor could get on with the rest of the estate administration, he or she would file this form.

As you will learn using this kit, beneficiaries of an estate must receive a written notice of their interest in the estate. If they cannot be identified or located, the executor is obviously not able to fulfill the requirement of serving the notice. The purpose of Form NC25 is to get the court's permission to go ahead without serving the person who cannot be identified or located.

Follow these steps to fill in your Form NC25:

1. Fill in the court file number from Form NC1.

2. Fill in the estate name exactly as you did on Form NC1.

3. Fill in the name of the deponent, which should be the executor.

4. Do not change the paragraph that appears in all capital letters.

5. In paragraph 1, you must describe your right to apply to the court for probate. The answer that appears in the sample document is that you are the executor named in the will. If this is the case, you do not have to change it. If the situation is slightly different, you must tweak this paragraph. For example, if there are co-executors, that must be described. If the first-named executor has renounced, that must be described. Paragraph 1 must match the description you gave at the beginning of your Form NC2 affidavit.

6. Do not change paragraphs 2 and 3.

7. In paragraph 4, describe any beneficiaries that are unknown. This is different from beneficiaries whose identities are known but who cannot be found. This paragraph refers to a beneficiary whose identity is not known. It is rare that an executor needs to use paragraph 4.

8. In paragraph 5, describe any beneficiaries whose identities are known but whom you have been unable to locate.

9. In paragraph 6, describe what you have done to identify or locate the beneficiaries. Some ideas are advertising in the newspaper, making enquiries at former workplaces of the beneficiary or the deceased, and telephoning family members.

10. Do not change paragraphs 7, 8, and 9.

11. Take your document to a Commissioner for Oaths.

12. Sign your document over the line that says "deponent" when you are in front of the Commissioner for Oaths.

13. The Commissioner will fill in the date and place of signing and will sign and stamp your document.

See Sample 16 for a sample of Form NC25.

Sample 16
Form NC25

NC25

COURT FILE NUMBER

ESTATE NAME   Samuel Winston France, a.k.a. Sammy France

DOCUMENT   **Affidavit regarding missing or unknown beneficiaries**

DEPONENT'S NAME   Lillian France

THE DEPONENT SWEARS UNDER OATH OR AFFIRMS THAT THE INFORMATION IN THIS AFFIDAVIT IS WITHIN THE DEPONENT'S KNOWLEDGE AND IS TRUE. WHERE THE INFORMATION IS BASED ON ADVICE OR INFORMATION AND BELIEF, THIS IS STATED.

Applicant

1. The applicant is entitled to apply for a grant because the applicant is the executor and trustee named in the deceased's Will.

2. The applicant has applied for a grant of probate.

3. The applicant cannot fully complete Schedule 4 nor provide a complete set of notices to beneficiaries.

Unknown beneficiaries

4. These beneficiaries are unknown to the applicant:

    4.1 _____

Missing beneficiaries

5. These beneficiaries cannot yet be located:

    5.1   June France _____

Enquiries

6. The applicant has made these enquiries to ascertain and find the beneficiaries:

    6.1   Placed advertisement in provincial newspapers; asked all relatives if they know whereabouts

Undertakings

7. The applicant undertakes:

    7.1 to advise the court as soon as they have ascertained or found the beneficiaries, and

    7.2 to provide the clerk with the notices to beneficiaries at that time.

8. The applicant believes that it is in the best interest of the estate to begin its administration immediately.

Prayer

9. That this Court grant the application for a grant of probate without Schedule 4 being fully completed and without sending all the notices to beneficiaries.

SWORN OR AFFIRMED BY THE DEPONENT BEFORE A COMMISSIONER FOR OATHS AT _____ Edmonton _____, ALBERTA ON _____ December 15, 2011 _____.

_____
Deponent

_____
Commissioner's Name

_____
Appointment Expiry Date

7

How to Prepare the Form NC7 Inventory

Form NC7 Inventory of property and debts is required for every application for probate, and administration or administration with will annexed (which are covered in Chapter 8).

Your job as an executor or administrator is to use the form to give a snapshot of the deceased's financial situation on the day he or she died. This means that every value you put into the Inventory must be the value of the asset or debt on the day that the deceased died. The Inventory is prepared on Form NC7, and you will find both a blank NC7 on the CD-ROM and a sample completed NC7 (shown in Sample 17).

Your first task to complete the inventory is finding out what assets and debts the deceased had and documenting them. You will have to visit, write, or call a number of people and places to get information. In each case, you should be prepared to provide —

- a copy of the death certificate to prove that the owner of the property is deceased;

- a copy of the will to prove that you are the appointed representative; and

- your personal identification.

In some cases, you will be asked to agree to send a copy of the Grant of Probate (for executors) or the Grant of Administration (for

70

Sample 17
Form NC7

ESTATE NAME   Amelia Jane Lockheart

DOCUMENT   **Schedule 5: Inventory of property and debts**

VALUE OF ESTATE IN ALBERTA

Land and buildings (net of encumbrances)	$371,500.00
Other property (gross)	$388,686.23
Gross value of estate	$760,186.23
Debts (excluding encumbrances of land)	$23,126.58
Net value of estate	$737,059.65

PROPERTY

LAND AND BUILDINGS

Description:	Plan 1234, Block 123, Lot 12
Gross value:	$400,000
Encumbrances:	($78,500)
Net value:	$321,500

Description:	Plan 4321, Block 321, Lot 21
Gross value:	$50,000
Encumbrances:	$nil
Net value:	$50,000

OTHER PROPERTY

Description:	Savings Account # 12345-67 CIBC, Lethbridge
Gross value:	$8,665.24

Description:	Chequing Account #67543-21 TD Canada Trust, Lethbridge
Gross value:	$10,258.99

Description:	GIC #555-3333-666 2.1%, matures December 31, 2015 TD Canada Trust, Lethbridge Principal $100,000 and interest of $562
Gross value:	$100,562

Sample 17 — Continued

| Description: | Life insurance policy #123456789 Great-West Life Assurance Co. |
| Gross value: | $250,000 |

| Description: | Canada Pension Plan death benefit |
| Gross value: | $2,500 |

| Description: | Local Authorities Pension Plan (LAPP) Death benefit |
| Gross value: | $7,500 |

| Description: | 2005 Ford Mustang VIN 123456789111222 |
| Gross value: | $9,000 |

| Description: | Household and personal goods |
| Gross value: | $200 |

TOTAL VALUE OF PROPERTY $760,186.23

DEBTS

Description:	Funeral expenses	
	Funeral home	$7,500
	Obituary	$500
	Flowers	$1,000
	Reception	$2,875
Value:	$11,875.00	

| Description: | Visa credit card #987 9876 9876 |
| Value: | $3,015.87 |

| Description: | Income tax for 2010 (estimate) |
| Value: | $8,235.71 |

TOTAL VALUE OF DEBTS $23,126.58

NET VALUE OF ESTATE $737,059.65

administrators) once it is issued. Gathering information for the Inventory is usually harder for administrators than for executors because there is no will to support you as you try to gather information before your application. Some people may refuse to cooperate with you, and you will have to estimate values.

If you are the spouse of the deceased, you may already be familiar with the details of the deceased's financial affairs. For example, you may already know where he or she banked, and whether he or she had life insurance. If you do not already have this information, you will have to look for it.

This involves looking through the deceased's papers in his or her home and any safety deposit boxes he or she might have rented. As more and more people rely on computers to do banking and other transactions, it becomes more difficult for executors to gain access to information. There is no one logical place to look. Here are some of the things you should be looking for:

- Bank statements and/or bankbooks for accounts, investments, loans, and lines of credit

- Statements from investment advisors

- Copies of insurance policies or letters from insurance companies

- Statements from private pensions

- Statements or notices from government programs such as Old Age Security, Canada Pension Plan, or Assured Income for the Severely Handicapped

- Original share certificates

- Copies of deeds to land

- Property tax statement from the city or county

- Recent income tax returns and statements of assessment

- Pay stubs

- Any T-slips, such as T4 or T5

- Unpaid bills

- Credit card statements

- Statements or letters from finance companies

- Appraisals for valuable artwork, collections, jewelry, etc.

- "Pink slips" for vehicles

- Any bills of sale that show the purchase of vehicles, trailers, boats, RVs, campers, quads, snowmobiles, etc.

- Any logins and passwords for online accounts

Also make sure that you find the deceased's driver's license, social insurance card, credit cards, passport, Alberta Health Care card, and any other personal identification, and make sure that you keep them in a secure, private place until you can deal with them. You are now the guardian of the deceased's privacy.

1. Contacting Banks, Insurance Companies, Etc.

Once you have compiled all the statements and policies you can find, you will have to write to each of the banks, investment companies, insurance companies, etc. You are trying to find out the following about each account or investment:

- Whether the account still existed on the date of the deceased's death

- If so, what was the balance at the date of death (note that with an account it should be a credit balance, but with a credit card you should expect a debit balance, or an amount owing)

- Whether the account was held in joint names with anyone else

- With insurance policies, you also need to know who is named as the beneficiary of the policy

Your letter serves two purposes. One is to officially notify the bank or company of the death of the deceased. The other is to find out the information listed above. You should include a notarial copy of the will and the Funeral Director's Statement of Death (or a death certificate) with each letter to prove that you have the right to ask for this confidential information. There are sample letters included on the CD-ROM for this purpose which you can personalize to suit your situation. Make sure you have included the correct information and removed the parts of the letters that do not apply to your situation.

Keep a copy of every letter you send out, making sure that the date on the letters is accurate.

Get your letters in the mail as soon as possible, because it will take weeks in some cases to get a reply. If you have not heard anything within two weeks, follow up your letter with a telephone call or an in-person visit. For your own protection, get all of their responses in writing, whether you get an original letter, a fax, or an email.

Sample letters to an insurance company, a credit card company, and a bank are provided on the CD-ROM.

In the case of electronic bill payments and banking, if an executor is unable to find logins and passwords, etc., he or she can contact a head office or main branch where the deceased did his or her banking.

The executor will have to provide identification and proof of the account holder's death. The bank is unlikely to provide access to an online account, as it will not have a record of the account holder's PIN. The executor should request the account be frozen (assuming there is no joint account holder) and request a printout of the account (a statement). The statement should go back far enough that the executor will be sure to spot regular debits and credits; even those that only happen once a year.

An executor can arrange with a banking officer to review any pre-made (autopay) arrangements. Sometimes this is the only way for an executor to identify to whom payments are being made. If automatic debits are for loan payments, the lender should be contacted directly to request they be stopped. Services such as Internet, cellphones, and utilities should also be cancelled directly with providers.

One way to ensure that automatic debits are stopped is to ask the bank to freeze the account until you have a chance to identify all the automatic transactions. Once bills are no longer being paid, providers or lenders who haven't heard from an executor will get in touch.

2. Obtaining Values

There are many assets for which you will have to assign a value. As you will find, it is impossible to please everyone on an estate, and you should back up your findings with paperwork whenever possible. That way, if anyone believes you are selling an asset too cheaply or valuing it too highly, you can show them how you arrived at its value. In this chapter, you will find some ideas for placing a value on estate items.

2.1 Finding real estate values

For homes, cottages, farmland, vacant land, and revenue properties, find values by doing one of the following —

- get an appraisal by a qualified appraiser. This is especially important for farm or other rural property;

- refer to the most recent tax assessment notice; or

- get at least two estimates from experienced realtors who are not in any way connected to the estate.

If real estate is jointly owned (not tenants-in-common) with anyone else, make sure you read section **2.8** about joint property.

Mines and minerals titles and leases are shown under real estate on Form NC7, but obviously they cannot be valued in the same way as other real estate. If there is a mineral title that has not produced any revenue for the last five years, you will probably assign it a value of $1. The best way to value mineral interests that are producing revenue is to multiply the last year's revenue by five years and use that amount as the value. For example, if the mineral lease produced $5,200 in 2010 (the last full year), express the value as:

$5,200 x 5 = $26,000.

2.2 Financial instruments

For bank accounts, investment portfolios, mutual funds, and any other financial instruments, request a statement from the financial institution. These accounts often contain stocks and bonds, but you do not need to evaluate each stock or bond separately. It is enough to put down the value of the entire portfolio. Use the sample letter to a bank on the CD-ROM and customize it to obtain information.

Make sure that you determine the value of the account on the date of death. If you are using a regular statement that is produced monthly or quarterly, the final balance is not likely to coincide with the date of death. If you cannot obtain a statement for the date of death, you will have to go through the statement to find the entry that is the closest to the date of death in order to use that entry as the cutoff entry and date.

If any accounts are jointly owned with another person, make sure you read section **2.8** about joint property ownership.

2.3 GICs

Guaranteed Investment Certificates (GICs) and term deposits are un-like other accounts in that they earn interest. Usually the interest is either paid once a year, or is not paid at all until the GIC matures. When you make enquiries at the bank, make sure you find out both the principal amount of the GIC and the amount of interest that has been earned but not yet paid to the deceased.

2.4 Stocks and shares

As mentioned above, stocks and shares do not have to be valued individu-ally if they are part of a portfolio that is managed by a money manager for the deceased. However, if the deceased owned individual stocks, they must be valued separately. You will know if the deceased owned these because you will find the actual paper certificates for the shares.

To find the values for these, you may use a website that gives stock values. There are several of them on the Internet, many of which are free to use. Make sure that you are getting the value in Canadian dollars. Also make sure you get the price as of the date of death. That usually means clicking on "historical search" on the site and entering the specific date.

Another method of finding stock values is to look in newspapers dated the same day as the date of death and find the stocks in the financial pages listing. Of course, if you know a broker or financial advisor, you may ask him or her to help you find the values.

Don't worry about what the stocks will be worth later; this will be dealt with in the final accounting. Inventory values need to be the values at the date of death.

2.5   Canada Savings Bonds

Canada Savings Bonds may be quickly and easily valued by checking the Government of Canada site at www.csb.gc.ca. If this is not available to you, check with a financial planner, broker, or banking officer by taking the original Bonds to them.

2.6   Vehicles

Members of Alberta Motor Association may obtain free vehicle book values through their AMA membership. Another way to value a vehicle is to buy a weekly magazine such as *Auto Trader* or *Bargain Finder* and find similar vehicles. This also works well for recreational vehicles, snowmobiles, quads, mountain bikes, trailers, boats, and motorcycles.

2.7   Antiques, artwork, collections, jewelry

These types of assets are the most difficult to valuate. The best method is to take clear, detailed photographs of the asset in question and take the photos around to dealers or shops that specialize in that type of asset. For example, you might take a collection of hockey cards to a sports collectibles and memorabilia shop. If you do not live in a larger centre where you have easy access to these shops, you can write to them enclosing your photos or scan the photos and email them to the shops or dealers.

Finding a similar item on eBay is not a very reliable method of valuing an asset.

2.8   Joint property

Property of any kind that is held in joint tenancy between two or more people is not included in Form NC7. Joint ownership gives a legal right to the surviving joint owner to own the entire account, so there is nothing to be recorded for the person who passes away. Be careful not to assume that just because there are two names on an asset that it is jointly owned. It is possible to have two or more names on a title to land, for example, without there being joint ownership. Always double check this by doing an up-to-date search at the Land Titles Office or inquiring at the bank about the ownership of an account.

3.   Beneficiary Designations

When looking at the deceased's financial statements, be sure to identify which of his or her accounts and investments are registered. The most common registered accounts are Registered Retirement Savings Plans (RRSPs) and Registered Retirement Income Funds (RRIFs). Whenever you find a registered account, you must find out who has been named beneficiary of the funds.

Registered funds normally do not form part of the estate and are not to be included in Form NC7. However, you should include the registered funds if —

- the named beneficiary is the deceased's estate; or

- the named beneficiary is someone who passed away before the deceased did.

If there is an RRSP or RRIF (or any other registered fund) being included in Form NC7, make sure that the following is recorded:

- Name of bank or investment house

- Plan number

- The full amount of the payout

The tax payable on registered funds being paid out to a beneficiary is payable by the estate, even when the estate does not receive any of the registered money. You must show this under "Debts" on Form NC7. For example, the deceased owned an RRSP with $50,000 in it. The beneficiary is the deceased's daughter. The daughter is therefore entitled to the entire $50,000.

This is not a situation in which the RRSP can be rolled over on a tax-deferred basis. The law says that the RRSP is deemed to have been cashed in one minute before the deceased died, so at that point, tax is payable on the RRSP. If the tax liability on the $50,000 is $20,000, that $20,000 has to come out of other assets in the estate, not from the RRSP. Therefore, you would not put the $50,000 on your Form NC7, but you would include the $20,000 tax liability.

If the deceased owned an RESP that names one of his/her children or grandchildren as the beneficiary of the plan, the RESP does not work like RRSPs or RRIFs. In fact, it operates in a very different way. Find out from the bank that is holding the RESP whether there is a successor plan owner. This refers to a person who was designated by the deceased to run the account in his place. If there is a successor plan owner (also called successor director) then you do not list the RESP on Form NC7. If there is no successor plan owner, the RESP will likely be collapsed and form part of the deceased's estate, so you should list it on the form with other financial assets.

Another common asset that has a beneficiary designation is a life insurance policy. If the beneficiary named on a life insurance policy is the estate, then you must include the full pay-out value on the form. Remember to get an up-to-date number from the insurance company to ensure that you are recording any income that has accrued to the policy. There is no tax arising automatically from the payment of life insurance, so there is no corresponding debt to be included in the debts section.

If you're recording a life insurance policy on Form NC7, make sure to include —

- the name of the company;
- the policy number;
- the type of insurance plan (e.g. group, life, joint-and-last-to-die, etc.); and
- the amount of the payout.

4. Ascertaining Debts

A mistake that many executors and administrators make is to leave debts and bills off the Inventory because they have already paid the bills themselves after the deceased died. Those bills still have to be included. Always remember the rule that you must show the bills that were in existence on the day the deceased died. Whether or not you have paid them since is irrelevant to the Inventory.

You should take a proactive approach to finding out what debts are out there. You may have to make inquiries or do searches, in addition to advertising for creditors and claimants (see Chapter 13 for more on that topic). Some of the inquiries you might want to make include the following —

- If the deceased was paying child support, find out whether there are any arrears owing and whether the ongoing support obligations continue after the deceased's death

- Look through the deceased's personal papers to find out what you can about lines of credit at the bank, credit cards, car loans, finance companies, etc.

- Write to credit card companies to find out card balances

- Read any leases the deceased had signed to understand what must be paid to terminate the lease

- Find out what is owing for electricity, water, cable, telephone, and Internet service

- If the deceased passed away in a hospital or hospice, find out whether there is any amount owing for ambulance or health services

- If the deceased had a mortgage, find out whether it was life insured

- Find out whether the deceased was making car payments and how much is still owed

- If someone alleges a debt owed by the deceased, find out whether it is statute-barred (i.e., incurred too long ago to be collectible)

- If anyone asks for payment for services rendered to the deceased, such as housekeeping, yard work, or health-care services, find out whether there is a written contract

- If a charitable organization claims that the deceased had promised a donation, make sure there is a written agreement signed by the deceased

- If the deceased was in the middle of a divorce, find out whether the issues surrounding division of property had been settled

- If the deceased operated a business as an unincorporated sole proprietor, review the business books to find out what is outstanding

- If the deceased owned a corporation, find out whether there is a buy-sell agreement

No matter what bill you're looking into, you should always understand the interest rate on any debt owed by the deceased.

5. Which Expenses for the Executor and Other Family Members Are Included?

No expenses for the family of the deceased or the family of the executor should be included in the inventory or repaid from the estate unless they were requested by the executor or incurred as a direct result of carrying out an estate duty. Also do not include the cost of anyone attending the funeral. People must do that at their own cost, even the family of the deceased. Family members will typically request reimbursement for flights, hotels, and meals, but these are not to be included.

Legitimate executor's expenses include —

- Long distance phone calls to financial institutions, beneficiaries, etc.

- Faxing or photocopying of estate paperwork

- Mileage and parking costs when the executor is on estate business, such as seeing the lawyer or accountant or filing documents at the courthouse

- Filing and search fees

- Postage

If the executor must travel to carry out his or her executor's duties, then expenses may include the following things for the executor (but not for his/her family or friends):

- Reasonable hotel costs

- Reasonable meals for the executor

- Reasonable transportation costs

If the executor has had to pay estate expenses while waiting for estate funds to become available, then expenses may include reimbursement for any bills paid on behalf of the estate, such as funeral costs.

6. What about a Breakdown of Funeral Expenses?

A breakdown of funeral expenses is required if the total cost of the funeral was $10,000 or more, but most executors will include a breakdown even if the cost was less than that. By doing so, they can show family members how estate money was spent. In the breakdown, list how much money was spent on:

- funeral home services

- cremation

- burial

- casket or urn

- plot or niche

- transportation of the body or remains

- headstone or plaque and engraving

- flowers

- obituary

- notices or cards

- church or hall rental

- funeral lunch, reception, or wake

- minister or rabbi

- music or singer

- any other expenses directly required for the funeral
- GST

7.   What to Do about Loans to the Deceased's Kids

If the deceased had made a loan to one or more of his or her children, or had given them large sums of money, these are considered advances to the children of part of their inheritance. On the NC7 Inventory, you will list each loan or advance as a receivable owed to the deceased.

Read the will to see if it says anything about forgiving loans to the children. If the will says that the deceased wanted to forgive the loan, then do not list it as a receivable. If there is nothing mentioned about forgiving it, then the amount must be deducted from the amount you will pay to the child who had the advance.

If the amount loaned to a child is more than the child is supposed to inherit, the executor or administrator should check to see whether there is a clause in the will forgiving the loan. Assuming there is no such clause, the executor should list the amount by which the loan exceeds the inheritance as a receivable to the estate.

8.   Completing the Summary Section of the Inventory

At the top of Form NC7, you will see a summary of the estate (shown below). You are asked to list all of the assets of the deceased, which gives you the gross value of the estate, then to list and subtract the debts, which gives you the net value of the estate. Although this section appears on the form first, it should be the last section you complete as it summarizes the rest of the document.

VALUE OF ESTATE IN ALBERTA

Land and buildings (net of encumbrances) $

Other property (gross) $

Gross value of estate $

Debts (excluding encumbrances of land) $

Net value of estate $

When you complete the "Land and buildings" section, total up all real estate values, then subtract any mortgages or liens; this will give you the net value of the real estate. Transfer the net value to the first line of the summary. There is more detail about this in the next section.

After completing the first section, move on to the "Other property" section. When you have finished that, transfer the number to the second line of the summary.

Add together the "Land and buildings" value and the "Other property" value. This will give you the gross value of the estate, and represents the value of the assets before taxes, funeral costs, and other expenses are subtracted. Put this number on the third line of the summary.

Move on to the "Debts" section and fill in all the debts of the deceased. Add them up and transfer the number to the fourth line of the summary.

At this point, you have all the numbers you need for the summary. Subtract the debts from the gross value of the estate. This will give you the net value of the estate, which you should put into the last line of the summary. You will notice that you also need to put the summary numbers into the bottom of the Inventory.

Refer to Sample 17 earlier in this chapter and on the CD-ROM to see how the numbers in the summary are found.

9. Completing the Real Estate Section of the Inventory

In the Land and Buildings section of the form, you will list all real property, which includes homes, land, cottages, commercial buildings, and mines and minerals titles, as long as they are in the name of the deceased. If the deceased owned a part of a property as a tenant-in-common, include only the deceased's part of the value of the property.

Do not include any property that is owned by a corporation, even if the corporation is fully owned by the deceased. Do not include property that the deceased owned as a joint tenant.

List each property separately by cutting and pasting these four lines for each property:

Description:
Gross value: $
Encumbrances: $
Net value: $

The gross value is the fair market value or selling price of the property. The word "encumbrances" refers to mortgages (whether first, second, third, or so on) and lines of credit that will be subtracted from the value of the property. If the mortgage is life insured, you do not have to include it because it will not reduce the value of the property. The net value is the selling price less the mortgage.

10. Completing the "Other Property" Section of the Inventory

In this part of the inventory, you will list all assets belonging to the deceased that are not real property. This includes:

- Bank accounts
- Term deposits and GICs
- Investments
- Canada Savings Bonds
- Insurance payable to the estate
- Vehicles and boats
- Shares of a business
- Other business interests such as shareholder loans
- Share certificates

- Collections and personal goods
- Money owed to the deceased
- CPP death benefit and other pension benefits

As digital assets grow in popularity, businesses have sprung up that allow individuals to register and record their assets online. This industry is in its infancy and is not yet widely used, and this service is only useful to an executor or administrator if the deceased person left some record of his or her account.

Organize the assets so that you have similar assets together. For example, list all of the bank accounts together. If you have a lengthy list of assets to include, you may wish to use the list in this section to create headings in your document, though that is not required. Remember that the values you include must be the values on the date of the deceased's death.

Cut and paste these two lines for each asset:

Description:
Gross value: $

Describe each asset in as much detail as possible. Remember that this inventory will be used for several purposes, all of which are going to be easier or more complete if you make your inventory entries as detailed as possible. The inventory will be used by beneficiaries, the estate accountant who has to do the tax returns, and by you when it is time to close the estate.

For bank accounts, include the —

- name of the bank,
- address of the bank,
- account number,
- account balance as of the deceased's date of death, and
- amount of interest (if any) that had accrued to the date of death but had not yet been paid.

For unregistered GICs and term deposits, include —

- name of the bank,
- address of the bank,
- account number,
- maturity date for the GIC or deposit,

- value of the GIC or deposit as of the deceased's date of death, and

- amount of interest, if any, that had accrued but not yet been paid as of the date of death.

For non-registered investment portfolios, you do not have to break it down into individual shares or bonds. Only break it down by individual account numbers. Include —

- name of bank or investment house,

- address of bank or investment house,

- account number,

- value of the entire portfolio as of the deceased's date of death, and

- amount of interest, if any, that had accrued but not yet been paid as of the date of death.

For Canada Savings Bonds, include —

- series number,

- bond number,

- maturity date,

- face value, and

- the amount of interest, if any, that had accrued but not yet been paid as of the date of death.

For life insurance payable to the estate, include —

- name of insurance company,

- policy number,

- face value of policy, and

- any additional amounts such as the savings component of a whole life policy.

For vehicles, boats, trailers, quads, snowmobiles, tractors, etc., include —

- year of the vehicle,

- make and model of the vehicle,

- VIN number or serial number, and

- Amount the vehicle could fetch if sold on the open market.

If the deceased owned an incorporated business, or part of one, include —

- number of shares held,
- description of shares (e.g. common, preferred, Class A, etc.),
- value per share, and
- total value of shares.

It can be quite difficult to place a value on shares of a private corporation. Usually the share value includes the value of all of the business's assets less the value of its liabilities. It would probably be wise to consult an accountant to fix the value of the shares.

The deceased might also have other business interests. This could be a share in a partnership, a shareholder loan, or a franchise. Again, you may wish to consult an accountant to arrive at the correct value. Don't forget to include the following:

- A description of the interest
- A value of the interest

For individual share certificates, include:

- Name of the company
- Certificate number
- CUSIP number (printed on the front of the certificate)
- Number of shares represented by the certificate
- Description of shares (e.g. common, preferred, Class A, etc.)
- Value per share
- Total value of the certificate

Household and personal goods, collections, jewelry, etc., are most often lumped together into a single heading of "household and personal goods." A nominal value such as $1,000 is then assigned to the whole group. You can do this as long as you separate out any valuable items and describe them individually. For example, you could bunch together all household goods, but have a separate entry for "Collection of seven Robert Bateman prints." You then assign a value to the print collection based on what the prints would fetch if sold on the open market.

If there is any money owed to the deceased, include:

- the name of the person or company who owes the money

- brief description such as "personal loan," "private mortgage," etc.

- interest rate of the loan, and

- balance of the loan outstanding as of the date of death.

For the CPP death benefit and any other pension benefits, include —

- name of the plan (e.g., CPP)

- brief description of the benefit (e.g., death benefit)

- pension or policy number, and

- amount of the benefit.

If the deceased was collecting Old Age Security, CPP, Alberta Senior's Benefit, Veteran's Benefit, Assured Income for the Severely Handicapped, or any other government benefit, you are entitled on behalf of the deceased's estate to keep the benefit payment for the month of death. Include it on the inventory if it has not yet been added to the bank balance.

Assets that are not named specifically in a will form part of the residue. They should be included in the inventory of the estate.

Once you have plugged in all of the values for the assets, you will add them up. This number is the gross value or total value of the estate. At the end of the "Other property" section of the inventory, you will see a place to type in this number. Transfer these final numbers to the summary section of the inventory.

11. Debts

In the next section of the inventory, you will list all of the debts and liabilities of the deceased that were outstanding on the date of death. Even if you have paid the bills since the deceased died, you must still list them. You will include —

- Funeral expenses

- Taxes for the current year and any other unpaid year

- Bank loans

- Loans from finance companies

- Lines of credit

- Credit cards

- Loans from friends or family

- Bills for the last month of the deceased's life, such as electricity, water, Internet, and phone
- Unpaid property tax
- Unpaid child support (if applicable)

For funeral expenses, include —

- A breakdown of the individual expenses, such as funeral home services, plot, obituary, flowers, etc.
- Total amount of funeral expenses

For income taxes, include —

- The year that the taxes were incurred
- Total amount of taxes owing, including interest

For loans from banks or finance companies and lines of credit, include —

- name of bank or other lender,
- amount of the loan unpaid as of the date of death,
- any interest accrued but not yet paid as of the date of death,
- interest rate on the loan, and
- any assets used as collateral.

For credit cards, include —

- name of the card (e.g., Visa),
- bank that issued the card,
- card number,
- balance outstanding as of the date of death, and
- any interest accrued but not yet paid as of the date of death.

For loans from friends or family members, include —

- name of lender and relationship to the deceased,
- address of the lender,
- amount of the loan outstanding as of the date of death,
- interest rate on the loan, and
- amount of interest accrued as of the date of death.

For the bills for the last month of the deceased's life, such as electricity, water, Internet, and phone, include —

- name of creditor (e.g., Telus),
- account number, and
- amount owing.

For unpaid property tax, include —

- civic (street) address of the property,
- legal description of the property, and
- amount of tax owing.

If the deceased was paying child support, the support may or may not be ongoing after his or her death. See section **4.** about ascertaining debts to determine whether there is still support owing. If there is, include the following —

- brief description of whether the amount refers to arrears or ongoing support (you may have to list both),
- name of child(ren),
- date of the court order,
- court that made the order (e.g., Queen's Bench of Alberta), and
- amount outstanding.

Note that you do not include mortgages in the debts section because you have already subtracted any mortgage amounts from the real property in the first section of the inventory.

12. Finishing Off the Inventory

At the end of each section, you will see lines to sum up the total amount of all property (this means real property and other property together) and the total of all debts. Fill in those lines and subtract the debts from the total value of property. The number you get is the net value of the estate.

TOTAL VALUE OF PROPERTY $
TOTAL VALUE OF DEBTS $
NET VALUE OF ESTATE $

The numbers you enter into these lines should be the same as the numbers you enter in the summary.

8

Grant of Administration (and Grant of Administration with Will Annexed)

1.   What If There Is No Will?

Unfortunately, many Albertans pass away without leaving behind a valid will. The person who takes charge of the deceased's estate when there is no will is called an administrator instead of an executor. There are some differences between an executor and an administrator, but most items in their job descriptions overlap. In Alberta, the proper name for either an executor or an administrator is personal representative. In this kit, we use the term "executor" when there is a will and "administrator" when there is no will.

If there is no valid will, you will be applying to the court for a Grant of Letters of Administration (also called Grant of Administration) instead of a Grant of Probate. You will still be sending a package of documents to the court, though some of the documents will be different than those used for an Application for Probate. The process to apply for a Grant of Administration will be reviewed in the next few chapters.

Much of the information in the earlier chapters about Grants of Probate will also apply to Grants of Administration. Note that you cannot apply for a Grant of Administration until at least 14 days after the deceased person has died.

2. Where Do I Search for a Will?

Although some provinces have a government registry for wills, Alberta does not. Therefore, there is no central place to look for wills and your search might end up being time consuming. The following are some places you might check:

- The safety deposit box at the deceased's bank
- The office of any lawyer that the deceased might have hired, even if the lawyer was hired for a real estate purchase or corporate matter
- The safe and filing cabinet in the deceased's house
- The safe and filing cabinet in the deceased's office or shop
- The drawers in the deceased's desk

If you do find the will, theoretically it will appoint an executor and the probate process can begin. If the will cannot be found, or if the will is found but for some reason the named executor cannot or will not act, proceed with the administration process.

3. Am I the Right Person to Apply for a Grant of Administration?

There is a system in place to determine who can apply for a Grant of Administration. Assuming there is no executor (otherwise you would be making a different application), the priorities are:

- First, a spouse, common-law spouse, or Adult Interdependent Partner of the deceased. An Adult Interdependent Partner (AIP) is Alberta's version of a common-law spouse. An AIP is any adult person, either of the opposite sex or same sex, who has lived with the deceased for at least three years in a relationship of interdependence (less than three years if they have a child together). The AIP cannot be anyone related to the deceased by blood. Nor can an AIP be a person who is paid a wage for living in the home, such as a housekeeper, caregiver, or nanny.
- Second, a child (by blood or adoption, but not a stepchild) of the deceased.
- Third, a grandchild of the deceased.
- Fourth, an issue of the deceased other than a child or grandchild. The word "issue" refers to blood descendants.

- Fifth, a parent of the deceased.

- Sixth, a brother or sister of the deceased.

- Seventh, a niece or nephew of the deceased, but only if that niece or nephew is a person who would inherit on intestacy. Inheriting on intestacy means that, because there is no valid will, the laws of Alberta dictate who is going to get a share of the estate, as set out in the chart at the end of this chapter.

Review this list before you start your application to make sure that you are the person with the highest priority. If you are not the person with the highest priority, you have to get a written renunciation from whoever has a higher priority than you do and everyone who has an equal priority to you. For example, a grandchild of the deceased cannot apply to be the administrator unless the spouse and all of the children (who have greater priority) and all of the other grandchildren (who have equal priority) state that they do not want to do it. The renunciation form is covered in Chapter 6, section **2.**

4. What Is a Grant of Administration with Will Annexed?

A Grant of Administration with Will Annexed is a type of Grant of Letters of Administration that is used when the deceased left a will, but for some reason, the executor appointment in that will is not valid. It could be because the person named as executor has died, cannot be found, has lost mental capacity, or refuses to act as executor. If there is no alternate executor named, the result is a will that is perfectly fine except that it does not have an executor.

In this case, the procedure is to have the court appoint someone else to stand in the executor's place and carry out the will. The application to the court is called Application for Letters of Administration with Will Annexed. See section **5.** on who is entitled to apply. There is a separate checklist for this application in Chapter 9.

5. Am I the Right Person to Apply for a Grant of Administration with Will Annexed?

The system of priority for who can apply for this grant is different from the list given above for Grants of Administration. This is because you would have a will to work from in this case. You only apply for this grant when the executor and alternate executor named in the will have passed away or are unable or unwilling to act as executor. The priority list looks like this:

- First in priority to apply is a residuary beneficiary of the estate of the deceased. If there are two or three residuary beneficiaries, each of them has an equal right to be the administrator. They will have to figure out among themselves who is ready, willing, and able to take on the job. Only in the case where none of the residuary beneficiaries wants to be the administrator do you look to the next person or persons on the list.

- Second in priority is a person who is receiving a life interest in the residue of the will. This refers to someone for whom the will sets up a trust for their lifetime.

- Third in priority is someone who would inherit a part of the residue of the estate only where the will does not completely dispose of everything in the estate (this is pretty rare).

- Fourth in priority is someone who is named in the will to receive a specific gift, such as a certain item or a specific sum of money.

- Fifth in priority is someone who is a contingent beneficiary of the residue of the estate. This refers to someone who will only inherit if a particular contingency happens. A common example would be where a gift is made to the testator's son, but if the son has predeceased, then the gift would go to the son's children. The contingent beneficiaries in this example are the son's children, as they inherit only if their father has passed away.

- Sixth in priority is someone who is a contingent beneficiary of a specific gift in the will.

Knowing who has priority involves interpreting the will and applying its terms to the deceased's family. If you cannot tell who has priority, it is a good idea to ask a lawyer for help. If you accidentally apply without having first priority, the court will either reject your application outright or put it aside until you get written renunciations from the people who are higher in priority.

6. What Does an Administrator Do?

The administrator does everything that an executor does. This kit contains a checklist of executor's duties which may also be used by an administrator. The difference is that an administrator has no authority until the court appoints him or her, whereas an executor can start on certain parts of the estate before the Grant of Probate is issued.

7. Who Gets the Estate When There Is No Will?

The *Intestate Succession Act* of Alberta states who gets the assets of the deceased if he or she did not leave a will. This will be important when you fill in the NC6 document, where you must determine what each beneficiary will receive. Note that beneficiaries do not get anything unless and until all debts and expenses of the estate have been paid. If an executor or administrator pays the beneficiaries without paying all the debts first, the executor or administrator might be required to pay those debts out of his or her own personal money.

Table 1 shows how an estate will be distributed in Alberta if there is no will. Use the left-hand column to find the scenario that fits the estate you are working on. Then refer to the right-hand column to see who gets the estate in that situation.

Note in this table that the word "spouse" is used to represent only legally married spouses and not common-law spouses. Common-law spouses are included in the group called "adult interdependent partners."

Also note that the word "children" refers to biological children, both legitimate and illegitimate, as well as legally adopted children. It does not include stepchildren who were not adopted by the deceased.

Table 1
Beneficiaries When There's No Will

The deceased had a spouse and no children.	The spouse gets the entire estate.
The deceased had an adult interdependent partner and no children.	The adult interdependent partner gets the entire estate.
The deceased had a spouse or an adult interdependent partner and one child.	The spouse or adult interdependent partner gets the first $40,000 of the estate, plus ½ of the rest. The child gets the other ½. If the child has died before the deceased, the child's children get the child's share, divided equally among them.
The deceased had a spouse or an adult interdependent partner and more than one child.	The spouse or adult interdependent partner gets the first $40,000 of the estate, plus 1/3 of the rest. The children share the other 2/3 equally. If any child has died before the deceased, the deceased child's children get his or her share, divided equally among them.

The deceased had both a spouse and an adult interdependent partner and was living with the adult interdependent partner.	The adult interdependent partner gets the first $40,000 and the rest is divided among the children as mentioned above. The spouse gets nothing.
The deceased had both a spouse and an adult interdependent partner but was not living with either of them.	Whoever lived last with the deceased gets the first $40,000 and the rest is divided as mentioned above.
The deceased did not have a spouse or an adult interdependent partner but had children.	The entire estate is divided equally among the children. If any child has died before the deceased, that child's share will be divided equally among his or her children.
The deceased had no spouse, adult interdependent partner, or issue.	The entire estate is divided equally between the deceased's parents. If only one parent is alive, that parent gets the whole estate.
The deceased had no spouse, adult interdependent partner, issue, or parents.	The entire estate is divided among the deceased's brothers and sisters. If any brother or sister has died before the deceased, that sibling's children will divide that sibling's share equally among them.
The deceased had no spouse, adult interdependent partner, issue, parents, brothers, or sisters.	The entire estate is divided among the deceased's nieces and nephews. If one has died before the deceased, the estate is shared only among those nieces and nephews who are alive.

9

How to Complete the Required Forms to Apply for Grant of Administration (or Grant of Administration with Will Annexed)

The forms needed to apply for a Grant of Administration are divided into required forms that are needed on all applications for Grants of Administration, and specialized forms which are only used when the facts of the case require them. In this chapter, you will find instructions for the required forms for both Grants of Administration and Grants of Administration with Will Annexed. Instructions for the specialized forms are found in Chapter 10.

1. Required Forms for Administration

The forms that are always required on every Application for Administration are:

- Form NC1 — Application
- Form NC2 — Affidavit
- Form NC3 — Schedule 1: Deceased
- Form NC5 — Schedule 3: Personal representative(s)
- Form NC6 — Schedule 4: Beneficiaries
- Form NC7 — Schedule 5: Inventory of property and debts
- Form NC21 — Notice to beneficiaries (intestacy) — see Chapter 12 for information this form

- Form NC27 — Affidavit of service

These forms will be discussed in detail in this chapter; samples and blank forms for you to use are available on the CD-ROM.

2. Required Forms for Administration with Will Annexed

An Application for Administration with Will Annexed is a cross between an Application for Probate and the usual Application for Administration. The only time you will apply for administration with will annexed is when there is a valid will but no valid executor appointment. This could be because the executor is deceased, has lost mental capacity, or refuses to act.

You will be applying as if you were the executor named in the will, and you will be responsible for carrying out the instructions in the will.

The forms that are always required on every Application for Administration with Will Annexed are:

- Form NC1 — Application
- Form NC2 — Affidavit
- Form NC3 — Schedule 1: Deceased
- Form NC4 — Schedule 2: Will
- Form NC5 — Schedule 3: Personal representative(s)
- Form NC6 — Schedule 4: Beneficiaries
- Form NC7 — Schedule 5: Inventory of property and debts
- The original will
- Either Form NC8 — Affidavit of witness to a will or Form NC9 — Affidavit of handwriting of deceased
- Form NC27 — Affidavit of service

You might have noticed that this list is very similar to the list for a regular application for administration with no will. This is why the instructions for these two applications appear together in this chapter. However, each type of application has its own checklist in this kit so you can double check that you have all the documents you need and none that you do not need.

3. Form NC1 (Admin) — Application for Grant of Administration and Application for Grant of Administration with Will Annexed

Form NC1 is a summary of your entire package of documents. It tells the court what the application is about, who is involved, and what you are asking the court to do. Though the title of this document is "Application," once you have completed all of your forms, they together with all your other documents are referred to as your Application for Administration.

Follow these steps to complete your Form NC1 (Admin):

1. Leave the space for "Court file number" blank as you will not know the number until you file your documents at the court.

2. Fill in the Judicial District according to the instructions in Chapter 4, section **2.** of this manual.

3. Fill in the deceased's full name as shown on the Certificate of Death or on the Funeral Director's Statement of Death. If the deceased also had a shortened version of his or her name that appears on any of the assets, include that as well. For example, if Richard Wilson had the name "Rick Wilson" on his bank account, you will need to include this nickname. You would enter his name as "RICHARD WILSON, ALSO KNOWN AS RICK WILSON."

4. Under "Procedure," fill in the word "Administration" or "Administration with Will Annexed" and delete the other choices. Note that throughout the forms, the executor or administrator of the estate is referred to as the "personal representative."

5. Under "Bond," fill in the correct response, which you can determine by reading Chapter 2, section **11.** Delete the responses that do not apply.

6. Under "Notices required," you must list the notices you will prepare as part of your application. Refer to Chapter 12 to find out which notices you need. You do not have to list the names of the people receiving them. Even if there are several people receiving an NC19 Notice to beneficiaries (residuary), you only have to list it once. Delete the names of the notices you are not using.

7. Indicate whether or not you are serving a copy of your Application on the Office of the Public Trustee. Simply fill in "yes" or "no." See Chapter 12, section **9.** if you are not sure whether you should serve them.

8. Fill in your full name under "Personal representative's name." Do not put in the names of alternate executors who are not applying or anyone who has renounced.

9. Under "Complete address for service," fill in one mailing address that can be used by the court or anyone else who needs to send you anything about the application.

10. You will see a signature line on the left hand side of the page and a date line on the right. Sign and date where indicated. Below the signature line, fill in your full name and address. If there is more than one person applying to be an executor, you must add a signature line and date line for that executor to use and fill in his or her information below the second signature line.

11. At the bottom of the page, you will see a signature line for the judge and the words "ORDER: ISSUE THE GRANT AS APPLIED FOR." Do not remove or change these words or the signature line.

See Sample 18 for an example of a completed form NC1.

For the Form NC1 document, you should also prepare a backer. Most documents do not need this, but Form NC1 is unique. Once the backer is prepared, use it like the back cover of a book. All of your documents with the exception of Form NC27 will be put together as described in Chapter 11 with the backer at the end to keep everything together.

Follow these steps to prepare the backer:

1. In the top right hand corner, put in the month and year that you are filing the documents.

2. Leave the court file number blank, as you will not know the number until you file the document at court.

3. Fill in the same judicial district as you filled in on Form NC1.

4. Fill in the name of the estate exactly the same as you did on Form NC1.

5. Instead of "Application for Probate," enter "Application for Administration" or "Application for Administration with Will Annexed."

6. At the bottom of the document, you will see the words "Filed by." Fill in your name (assuming you are the administrator), along with your full mailing address, telephone number, and fax number if you have one.

See Sample 4 for a sample backer.

Sample 18
Form NC1 (Administration)

NC1

COURT FILE NUMBER

COURT **Court of Queen's Bench of Alberta (Surrogate Matter)**

JUDICIAL DISTRICT Edmonton

ESTATE NAME Samuel Winston France, a.k.a. Sammy France

PROCEDURE **Application by the personal representative(s) for a grant of _____ administration _____**

BOND Not required

NOTICES REQUIRED NC21 Notice to beneficiary on intestacy
NC22 Notice to spouse/*Matrimonial Property Act*
NC23 Notice to spouse/*Dependants Relief Act*

COPY OF THE APPLICATION FILED WITH THE PUBLIC TRUSTEE'S OFFICE No

PERSONAL REPRESENTATIVE'S NAME Lillian France

COMPLETE ADDRESS FOR SERVICE ON THE PERSONAL REPRESENTATIVE 4550 – 450 Avenue
Edmonton, Alberta
T5T 5T5

_____   _____
Personal Representative   Date

Name: Lillian France
Complete address: 4550 – 450 Avenue, Edmonton, Alberta, T5T 5T5
Phone: 780-555-5555
Fax: N/A

ORDER: ISSUE THE GRANT AS APPLIED FOR

_____   _____
Justice of the Court of Queen's   Date
Bench of Alberta

4. Form NC2 — Affidavit (Administration)

An affidavit contains the facts and evidence needed by the court to process the application. The affidavit must be sworn by the administrator before a Commissioner for Oaths or Notary Public. If there are co-administrators, then both must sign and swear the document. Forms NC3 through NC7 are schedules to this affidavit and will later be attached to it.

Follow these steps to complete your Form NC2:

1. Leave the court file number blank until you file your documents at court.

2. Fill in the same judicial district as you did on Form NC1.

3. Fill in the estate name exactly as it appears on Form NC1.

4. Under "Document," make sure it says "administration" or "administration with will annexed."

5. The deponent is the person who is signing and swearing the Form NC2 Affidavit. This will always be the person who is going to act as administrator. If there is more than one administrator, list both names.

6. You will now move to the body of the affidavit, where the paragraphs are numbered.

7. In paragraph 1, you must explain your right to make the application for administration or for administration with will annexed. State that you are the person with the highest priority to apply. If there is anyone with higher or equal priority to you, state that they have renounced.

8. Under "Schedules attached," list Forms NC3 through NC7 using the number and name of each document. If you are applying for administration (with no will), delete the reference to Form NC4.

9. If you are applying for administration with will annexed, under "Documents attached," list the will (e.g., "Will of John James Smith dated January 10, 1998"). Also list Form NC8 Affidavit of witness to a will or Form NC9 Affidavit of handwriting.

10. In paragraph 3 (or 4 if any documents are attached), you must list the notices you are going to serve and delete the ones you won't serve. You do not need to include the names of the people who will be served. This list should match the list you made in Form NC1.

11. Do not change paragraph 4.

12. Fill in the place and date that the Form NC2 is being signed and sworn.

13. You will see a signature line with the word "deponent" below it. Remove the word "deponent" and put in your name. If there is more than one administrator, make a new signature line and put in that person's name. You do not need to put in a new signature line for the Commissioner for Oaths if both administrators swear the document at the same time.

See Sample 19 for a filled-out example of NC2.

5. Form NC3 — Schedule 1: Deceased

The purpose of Form NC3 is to give the court a full description of the deceased person and his or her family members.

Follow these steps to complete your Form NC3:

1. At the top of the page, add the name of the deceased exactly as it appears on your NC1 application.

2. Under "Name," fill in the deceased's name. If there is a will attached, the name should appear as it appears on the will.

3. In the following line, fill in any other names such as maiden name, other married names, or nicknames.

4. For the residence address, fill in the full street address and mailing address, including postal code. If the deceased passed away in a hospital or other facility but had a home that he or she usually lived in when not ill, fill in the address of the usual home, not the facility.

5. Fill in the deceased's exact date of birth and name the town/city and the province, state, or country. No street address is required.

6. Fill in the deceased's exact date of death and place of death. This does not refer to a hospital, care facility, or mailing address. It only requires the town/city and province, state, or country. If the deceased died away from home on a vacation or business trip, fill in the name of the city or town he or she was in when he or she died.

7. Fill in the province or state that the deceased usually lived in. This should in most cases be Alberta. If this is not your answer, reconsider whether you are applying in the right jurisdiction.

Sample 19
Form NC2 (Administration)

NC2

COURT FILE NUMBER

COURT **Court of Queen's Bench of Alberta (Surrogate Matter)**

JUDICIAL DISTRICT Edmonton

ESTATE NAME Samuel Winston France, a.k.a. Sammy France

DOCUMENT **Affidavit by the personal representative(s) on application for a grant of** ___administration___

DEPONENT'S NAME Lillian France

THE DEPONENT SWEARS UNDER OATH OR AFFIRMS THAT THE INFORMATION IN THIS AFFIDAVIT AND IN THE ATTACHED SCHEDULES IS WITHIN THE DEPONENT'S KNOWLEDGE AND IS TRUE. WHERE THE INFORMATION IS BASED ON ADVICE OR INFORMATION AND BELIEF, THIS IS STATED.

Applicant

1. The applicant is entitled to apply for a grant because the applicant is the person with the highest priority to apply .

Schedules Attached

2. The following schedules are part of this affidavit. They are correct to the deponent's information and belief.

   2.1 NC3 Schedule 1 Deceased
   2.2 NC5 Schedule 3 Personal representative
   2.3 NC6 Schedule 4 Beneficiaries
   2.4 NC7 Schedule 5 Inventory

Documents Attached

The schedules and documents that are part of this affidavit provide all the information required in this application by the *Surrogate Rules* and have been prepared by me.

Notices

3. The applicant will serve the following notices as required and in the manner prescribed by the *Surrogate Rules*.

   3.1 NC21 Notice(s) to beneficiaries (intestacy)
   3.2 NC22 Notice to spouse of deceased *Matrimonial Property Act*
   3.3 NC23 Notice to spouse/adult interdependent partner of deceased *Dependants Relief Act*

Sample 19 — Continued

4. The applicant will faithfully administer the estate of the deceased according to law and will give a true accounting of their administration to the persons entitled to it when lawfully required.

SWORN OR AFFIRMED BY THE DEPONENT BEFORE A COMMISSIONER FOR OATHS AT _____Edmonton_____, ALBERTA ON _____December 1, 2011_____ .

_____
Deponent

_____
Commissioner's Name

_____
Appointment Expiry Date

8. Next you will give information to the court about the members of the deceased's immediate family. Leave in the sentence about children being over 18 and not disabled (on page 2 of Sample 20). This puts the responsibility on you to point out any family members who are not over 18 or who are physically or mentally disabled.

9. Under the heading of "SPOUSE," if the deceased was legally married (not common law), fill in the spouse's full name and complete street and mailing address. If there is no legally married spouse, state "none."

10. Under the heading of "ADULT INTERDEPENDENT PARTNER," if the deceased lived in a common-law relationship, either opposite sex or same sex, fill in the partner's full name and complete street and mailing address. If there was no common-law partner, state "none" and delete the rest of the paragraphs under the ADULT INTERDEPENDENT PARTNER heading.

11. If you fill in a name under ADULT INTERDEPENDENT PARTNER, you must select one of the next three paragraphs to include in the document. The two that you do not select may be deleted. Choose one of the following —

   • In the paragraph that begins with "for a continuous period of not less than 3 years," fill in the date that the deceased began living with his/her partner and the date that they stopped living together. If they were still living together when the deceased died, you may say "on the death of the deceased" for the ending date,

   • In the paragraph that begins with "of some permanence of which there is a child," fill in the date that the deceased's child with his/her partner was born or adopted, or

   • In the paragraph that begins with "the adult interdependent partner entered into an agreement," fill in the date that the agreement was signed.

12. Check off whether the person named as the common-law partner (adult interdependent partner) is related to the deceased by blood or adoption.

13. Under the heading of "CHILDREN," you will see five lines of information starting with "name" and ending with "died leaving children." For each child of the deceased, regardless of age, you must supply all of this information. Cut and paste the questions as many times as you need to. If there are no children, simply state "none."

14. If a child of the deceased is 18 or older, under "Age" you may simply put "over 18." The purpose of this question is to identify minors.

15. If a child is a minor, fill in the exact birthday next to "date of birth."

16. You do not need to include birth dates for anyone who is 18 or older.

17. If a child of the deceased had died before the deceased, fill in the date that the child died.

18. If a child of the deceased had died before the deceased, fill in either "yes" or "no" to the question of whether that child died leaving children of his/her own (i.e., grandchildren of the deceased).

19. If no child of the deceased had passed away, you may remove the lines referring to the death of a child.

20. Under "FORMER SPOUSES," you only need to include —

    • any spouse to whom the deceased was legally married (not common law) and who was divorced from the deceased within the two years prior to the deceased's death, or

    • any spouse (legally married, not common law) who has been divorced from the deceased for more than two years, but the division of property or assets has not been finalized.

21. If there is no such spouse, you may simply say "none." If the family situation is complicated, for example with several children with different surnames, including the names of former spouses can be helpful to the court in figuring out who is who.

See Sample 20 for an example of a completed Form NC3.

6. Form NC4 — Schedule 2: Will

The purpose of Form NC4 is to summarize the information about the will that is being attached. If you are applying for a grant of administration because there is no will, you do not need to complete this form and you should make sure that it is not listed on your Form NC2 affidavit.

If you are applying for administration with will annexed, most of the information you will need for this form is included in the will itself. You will complete an NC4 even if the will you are probating is a handwritten will.

NC3

ESTATE NAME	Samuel Winston France, a.k.a. Sammy France
DOCUMENT	**Schedule 1: Deceased**

Name: Samuel Winston France
And any other name(s) by which known: Sammy France
Last residence address in full: 122 Apple Boulevard, Edmonton, Alberta, T5T 4T4
Date of birth: February 22, 1936
Place of birth: Calgary, Alberta
Date of death: October 1, 2011
Place of death: Calgary, Alberta
Habitual province/state of residence: Alberta

The deceased died Intestate. After a thorough search of all likely places, no testamentary paper of the deceased has been found.

IMMEDIATE FAMILY

Complete information or state none in each category.

[   ] SPOUSE
    Name (or state none, if applicable): _None_____
    Complete address: _____

[   ] ADULT INTERDEPENDENT PARTNER
    Name (or state none, if applicable): _None_____
    Complete address: _____

    [   ] the adult interdependent partner lived with the deceased in a relationship of interdependence
    [   ] for a continuous period of not less than 3 years commencing
        _____ and ending _____.
    [   ] of some permanence of which there is a child

        [   ] born _____
                 date
        [   ] adopted _____
                 date

    [   ] the adult interdependent partner entered into an adult interdependent partner agreement with the deceased which agreement is dated _____.

    The adult interdependent partner

    [   ] is
    [   ] is not

    related to the deceased by blood or adoption.

[X] CHILDREN
Except as otherwise provided, all of the deceased's children are over 18 years of age at the time of the deceased's death, and none is unable by reason of mental or physical disability to earn a livelihood.

Name (or state none, if applicable): Lillian France
Complete address: 4560 – 450 Avenue, Edmonton, Alberta, T5T 5T5
Age: Over 18

[X] FORMER SPOUSES (Who require notice under the *Matrimonial Property Act*)
Name (or state none, if applicable): Mirabelle France
Complete address: 555 Green Street, Airdrie, Alberta, T5T 4T4
Date of divorce: June 15, 2011

Follow these steps to complete your Form NC4:

1. Fill in the estate name exactly as it appears on your NC1 application.

2. Fill in the deceased's age on the day he or she signed the will. If the deceased was not yet 18 years old when he or she signed, you must explain why he or she was able to make a valid will while still a minor. Your choices are —

   • the deceased was married;

   • the deceased had an adult interdependent partner (i.e., common-law spouse);

   • the deceased had a child;

   • the deceased was in the Canadian Forces and was on active service; or

   • the deceased was a mariner or seaman.

3. Under "marriages," you need only mention marriages that occurred after the will was signed. If there was no such marriage, say "none" and remove all other words in this section. If the deceased did marry after the will was signed, fill in the full name of the spouse and the date of the marriage. You will note that you are also including the words "as contemplated in the will." Check the will to make sure that it contains a clause about being made in contemplation of marriage. If it does not, the will is void and cannot be sent to the court.

4. Fill in the name of the two witnesses to the will. If the will was handwritten and did not have witnesses, add the words "the will was handwritten and did not have witnesses."

5. Leave in the sentence that neither witness was a beneficiary or the spouse of a beneficiary. Check the will to make sure this is true. If not, change the wording to reflect the real situation. The will is still valid but the gift to the witness/beneficiary is not.

6. The last line to be filled in is asking about anything that was handwritten into the will at the time of signing or crossed out. If nothing was changed or added, fill in the words "There appear to be no erasures, changes, or other additions to the will." If there are handwritten changes, state what they are as briefly and clearly as you can. For example, "on the bottom of the last page of the will, the word June was crossed out and the word July was handwritten in right above it."

7. Print your document and attach it to the NC2 Affidavit.

See Sample 21 for an example of a completed Form NC4.

7. Form NC5 — Schedule 3: Personal Representative(s)

The purpose of Form NC5 is to give the court information about you and to establish your right to be the one to apply for administration. Remember that the phrase "personal representative" includes both executors and administrators. If there are two administrators, do not make a separate NC5; simply add one person's information below the other.

Follow these steps to complete your Form NC5:

1. Fill in the estate name exactly as it appears on your Form NC1.

2. Fill in the full legal name of the administrator(s).

3. Fill in the complete mailing addresses of the administrator(s) including postal code.

4. Under "Status," you must indicate why you are the right person to apply for administration or administration with will annexed. In almost every case, you will choose "the person with the highest priority to apply" as your reason for applying. If anyone renounced, make sure you say that here, as it is part of the reason you are able to apply.

5. Fill in your relationship to the deceased (e.g., spouse, sibling, friend).

6. Do not change the sentence regarding age, as you must be 18 years or older to apply to be an administrator.

7. If there is anyone with a greater or equal right to apply, you must fill in their name and relationship here. There would be someone with that kind of right if:

   • there is an executor named who is not applying for some reason, or

   • there is someone with a closer blood relationship than you to the deceased. For example, if you are a nephew but the deceased also left a spouse and children, you would have to put in the names of those people because they are more closely related than you are.

8. If somebody has renounced, list his or her name and attach a written, signed renunciation (Form NC12) to the NC2 Affidavit.

NC4

ESTATE NAME   Samuel Winston France, a.k.a. Sammy France

DOCUMENT   **Schedule 2: Will**

Date of will: August 12, 1991

Deceased's age at date of will: 56

Marriages of deceased subsequent to date of will: None

Adult interdependent partner agreements entered into by deceased subsequent to date of will: None

Name of first witness: Charlene Hightower

Name of second witness: Jim Middlemarch

Neither witness is a beneficiary or the spouse or adult interdependent partner of a beneficiary named in the will.

To the best of the personal representative(s) information and belief, this is the deceased's original last will.

The personal representative(s) have examined the will and observe that
_____ no handwritten changes were made to it _____.

9. Attach your completed Form NC5 to the Form NC2 Affidavit.

See Sample 22 for an example of a completed Form NC5.

8. Form NC6 — Schedule 4: Beneficiaries (Application for Administration Only)

When there is no will, Form NC6 is used to describe to the court who is going to get what from the estate according to Alberta's *Intestate Succession Act*. You should refer to Chapter 8, section **7.** to figure out how the Act applies to the individual people in the deceased's life.

Follow these steps to complete Form NC6:

1. Fill in the estate name exactly as it shows on your Form NC1 Application.

2. The six items to fill in, starting with "Name" down to "Section no. (intestacy)," must be repeated for each and every beneficiary of the estate. Depending on how many beneficiaries there are, this could make your Form NC6 very lengthy, but that is

Sample 22
Form NC5 (Administration)

NC5

ESTATE NAME   Samuel Winston France, a.k.a. Sammy France

DOCUMENT   **Schedule 3: Personal representative(s)**

Name(s): Lillian France

Complete address(es): 4550 – 450 Avenue, Edmonton, Alberta, T5T 5T5

Status: The person with the highest priority to apply

Relationship to deceased: Daughter

Age: over 18

Any persons with a prior or
equal right to apply: No

Renunciations attached: No

perfectly okay. You may cut and paste the six items before filling in any information.

3. Under "Name," fill in the full legal name of the beneficiary, not nicknames.

4. Fill in the relationship of the beneficiary to the deceased (e.g., child, sibling).

5. Fill in the complete mailing address and street address of the beneficiary.

6. Under "Age," you need only put in a specific age if the beneficiary was not yet 18 years old on the day the deceased died. If the beneficiary was 18 years old or older, fill in "over 18."

7. Under "Nature of gift," you should very briefly describe what portion of the residue of the estate the beneficiary is entitled to receive.

8. Fill in the section number of the *Intestate Succession Act* that gives the beneficiary the gift, using Table 2. Look up the scenario

you are dealing with on the right hand column, then use the section number listed on the left. You will see that different beneficiaries will have different section numbers.

9. Remember to repeat all of the above information for each beneficiary.

10. The last question on this form asks you to list any gifts that are void because the will was improperly witnessed. As this is irrelevant where there is no will, simply state "none."

Table 2
Section Numbers of Intestate Succession Act

Use this section number ...	... if this situation applies:
2	the deceased left a married spouse but no children
2	the deceased left an adult interdependent partner (AIP) but no children
3(2)(a)	the deceased left a married spouse or AIP and one child
3(2)(b)	the deceased left a married spouse or AIP and more than one child
3(3)	one of the deceased's children died before the deceased did, and the child left children of his/her own who will take his/her share
3.1(1)(a)	the deceased left both a married spouse and an AIP, and at the time of his/her death was living with the legally married spouse
3.1(1)(b)	the deceased left both a married spouse and an AIP, and at the time of his/her death was living with the AIP
4	the deceased left no spouse or AIP
5	the deceased left no spouse, AIP, or children
6	the deceased left no spouse, AIP, children, or parents
7	the deceased left no spouse, AIP, children, parents, or siblings
8	the deceased left no spouse, AIP, children, parents, siblings, nieces, or nephews

NC6

ESTATE NAME   Samuel Winston France, a.k.a. Sammy France

DOCUMENT   **Schedule 4: Beneficiaries**

Name(s): Lillian France

Relationship: Daughter

Complete address: 4550 – 450 Avenue, Edmonton, Alberta, T5T 5T5

Age: over 18

Nature of gift: 100% of estate

Para. no. will: 5

Section no. (intestacy): 4

Except as otherwise provided, all beneficiaries are mentally capable.

The following gifts are void because the beneficiary is a witness or the spouse or adult interdependent partner of a witness to the will:

9. Form NC6 (Annexed) — Schedule 4: Beneficiaries (Application for Administration with Will Annexed Only)

When you are applying for Administration with Will Annexed, Form NC6 is used to describe to the court who is going to get what under the will (and codicil, if applicable). You will have to read the will, then figure out how it applies to the individual people in the deceased's life.

Follow these steps to complete Form NC6:

1. Fill in the estate name exactly as it appears on your Form NC1 application.

2. The six items to fill in — starting with "Name" down to "Para. no will" — must be repeated for each and every beneficiary of the estate. Depending on the gifts set out in the will, this could make your NC6 very lengthy, but that is perfectly okay. You may cut and paste the six items before filling in any information.

3. Under "Name," fill in the full legal name of the beneficiary (not nicknames).

4. Fill in the relationship of the beneficiary to the deceased (e.g., child, sibling, friend). If the beneficiary is a charity, fill in "none."

5. Fill in the complete mailing address and street address of the beneficiary.

6. Under "Age," you need only put in a specific age if the beneficiary was not yet 18 years old on the day the deceased died. If the beneficiary was 18 years old or older, enter "over 18."

7. Under "Nature of gift," you should very briefly describe what the beneficiary is going to receive under the will. It is best to follow the wording of the will as closely as possible.

8. Fill in the paragraph number of the will that gives the beneficiary the gift.

9. Remember to repeat all of the above information for each beneficiary.

10. The last question on this form asks you to list any gifts that are void because the will was improperly witnessed. If there are no gifts to list, simply state "none." If the will was witnessed by a beneficiary or the spouse or common-law spouse of a beneficiary, any and all gifts to that beneficiary must be listed here as being void.

10. Form NC7 — Schedule 5: Inventory of Property and Debts

Because this form is the most complicated and time-consuming of all the forms, there is a separate chapter in this kit devoted to preparing it. See Chapter 7.

11. Form NC27 — Affidavit of Service

See Chapter 12, section **12.**, for step-by-step instructions on preparing Form NC27.

12. Notices to Beneficiaries

Because the choice of which notices to use is so important, Chapter 12 is devoted to a more thorough description of the notices. That chapter contains detailed instructions for completing each notice, so refer to it to decide which notices you need.

Go over Checklists 4 or 5 to ensure you have all the required documents for either an Application for Grant of Administration or for an Application for Grant of Administration with Will Annexed. Chapter 10 will go over any specialized documents you might also need.

Checklist 4
Documents Required on Every Application
for Grant of Administration — No Will Attached

Document	Done	Notes
Form NC1 — Application for administration		
Form NC2 — Affidavit by the personal representative(s) on application for a grant of administration		
Form NC3 — Schedule 1: Deceased		
Form NC5 — Schedule 3: Personal representative(s)		
Form NC6 — Schedule 4: Beneficiaries		
Form NC7 — Schedule 5: Inventory		
Form NC27 — Affidavit of service		

Checklist 5
Documents Required on Every Application
for Administration with Will Annexed

Document	Done	Notes
Original will		
Form NC1 — Application for administration with will annexed		
Form NC2 — Affidavit by the personal representative(s)		
Form NC3 — Schedule 1: Deceased		
Form NC4 — Schedule 2: Will		
Form NC5 — Schedule 3: Personal representative(s)		
Form NC6 — Schedule 4: Beneficiaries		
Form NC7 — Schedule 5: Inventory		
Form NC8 — Affidavit of witness to will (mark the back of the original will as Exhibit A to this affidavit) or Form NC9 (Affidavit of handwriting)		
Form NC27 — Affidavit of service		

10

How to Complete the Specialized Documents to Apply for a Grant of Administration (or Grant of Administration with Will Annexed)

The specialized forms that are not used in every application but might be needed for your situation are described in this chapter. Each section has clear instructions about who should use the forms described. They are:

- Form NC8 — Affidavit of witness to a will
- Form NC9 — Affidavit of handwriting of deceased
- Form NC15 — Renunciation of administration
- Form NC16 — Nomination and consent to appointment of personal representative
- Form NC17 — Affidavit to dispense with a bond
- Form NC18 — Consent to waive bond

1. Form NC8 — Affidavit of Witness to a Will

Use Form NC8 if —

- you are applying for a grant of administration with will annexed; and

- the will you are working with is a formal, typewritten will, not a will in the testator's own handwriting.

Form NC8 was described in detail in Chapter 5 of this kit. See Chapter 5, section **8.**, for the sample form as well as the step-by-step instructions. There is a blank form available on the CD.

2. Form NC9 — Affidavit of Handwriting of Deceased

Use Form NC9 if —

- you are applying for a grant of administration with will annexed, and

- the will you are working with is handwritten.

Form NC9 was explored in some detail in Chapter 6. The form is identical for an application for a Grant of Administration with Will Annexed. See Chapter 6 for the form itself as well as step-by-step instructions for its completion. There is a blank form available on the CD.

3. Form NC15 — Renunciation of Administration

In Chapter 6, you saw how to complete a renunciation of probate. In this chapter, we will look at renunciation of administration. This form is different because the right to apply for administration does not arise from a will.

Use Form NC15 if one of the following applies:

- you are applying for a grant of administration and someone else needs to renounce so you can take over as administrator;

- there is someone who has a greater right to apply for administration than the person who is applying but who does not want to; or

- there is someone with equal priority to apply for administration as the person who is applying, but who does not wish to apply.

Follow these steps to fill in your Form NC15 (see Sample 24):

1. Fill in the estate name exactly as you did on Form NC1.

2. Fill in the name and complete address, including postal code, of the person who is going to renounce.

3. In paragraph 1, fill in the name of the deceased.

4. In paragraph 2, state the relationship of the renouncing person to the deceased (e.g., spouse, child, sibling).

5. Do not change paragraph 3.

6. Fill in the date that the person signed the form.

7. The person renouncing must sign on the signature line on the left hand side of the page in front of a witness.

8. The witness must sign above the signature line on the right hand side of the page.

9. Form NC15 has a second page. The second page is titled NC11, but it must be stapled to and kept with the NC15. The second page is the proof that the renunciation was properly signed. Form NC11 must be signed and sworn by the witness in front of a Commissioner for Oaths.

10. At the top of Form NC11, fill in the estate name exactly as you did on Form NC1.

11. The deponent is the witness who signed on the right hand side of Form NC15. Fill in the name of the deponent.

12. Fill in the date that the deponent signs.

13. Do not change the sentence that appears in all capital letters.

14. In paragraph 1, fill in the name of the person who signed Form NC15 (the person renouncing, not the witness).

15. In paragraph 2, fill in the same name again, then fill in the name of the city, town, or hamlet in Alberta where Form NC15 was signed (this may be different from where Form NC11 is signed).

16. Choose between the two forms of paragraph 3. Use the first one if the person signing Form NC15 is someone the witness/deponent knows personally. Use the second one if the person signing Form NC15 is someone that the witness/deponent does not know personally but who he or she can identify by looking at his/her identification. Delete the version of paragraph 3 that you do not use.

17. In paragraph 4, fill in the name of the person who renounced in Form NC15.

18. The Commissioner for Oaths will fill in the place and date that the Form NC11 is signed.

19. The deponent/witness must sign on the signature line on the left hand side of Form NC11 only when he or she is in front of a Commissioner for Oaths.

20. The Commissioner for Oaths will sign, date, and stamp the document on the right hand side of the page.

4. Form NC16 — Nomination and Consent to Appointment of Personal Representative

Form NC16 serves a similar purpose to Form NC15, except it also allows the person renouncing to nominate a person to act as administrator. This arrangement is sometimes made among family members when they get together and agree as to which of them will manage the estate. The document is to be signed by anyone who is renouncing, whether they are an executor, beneficiary, or family member.

Use Form NC16 if —

- You are applying for a grant of administration or a grant of administration with will annexed;

- A person with a right to apply for administration, or administration with will annexed wants to give up ("renounce") that right to apply, and

- The person renouncing wants to nominate a particular person to be the applicant instead.

Follow these steps to complete Form NC16:

1. Fill in the estate name exactly as you did on Form NC1.

2. Fill in the name and complete address, including postal code, of the person who is nominating an administrator.

3. There are two sets of paragraphs 1 and 2. You must choose the one that suits your situation. Choose the first set if there is a will in which an executor has been named and that executor is renouncing. Choose the second if there is no will. Delete the set that you do not use.

4. In paragraph 1, fill in the name of the deceased.

5. If you are using the first set, also fill in the name of the executor who was named and is renouncing.

6. If you are using the second set, state the nominating person's relationship to the deceased (e.g., spouse, child, sibling) in paragraph 2.

7. In paragraph 3, describe why the nominating person is involved in the estate. For example, is he or she named in the will? Is he or she a beneficiary on intestacy?

8. In paragraph 4, fill in the name of the person who is being nominated as an administrator. Note that there are two versions of paragraph 4 and you must choose the one that suits your situation. Delete the one that does not apply.

Sample 24
Form NC15 + NC11

NC15

ESTATE NAME	William Brown, a.k.a Bill Brown
DOCUMENT	**Renunciation of administration**
NAME	Jerry Stein
COMPLETE ADDRESS	1249 White Avenue, Calgary, Alberta, T5T 5T5

1. The deceased, _____William Brown_____, died intestate.

2. I am entitled to apply for a grant of administration under the Surrogate Rules because I am the deceased's _____nephew_____.

3. I renounce all my right and title to a grant of administration of the deceased's property.

SIGNED ON _____October 2, 2011_____.

_____*Jerry Stein*_____   _____*I.M. Witness*_____
Signature   Witness

This document must have Form NC11 attached.

Sample 24 — Continued

NC11

ESTATE NAME	Samuel Winston France, a.k.a. Sammy France
DOCUMENT	**Affidavit of Witness to Signature on Renunciation of administration**
DEPONENT'S NAME	I.M. Witness

THE DEPONENT SWEARS UNDER OATH OR AFFIRMS THAT THE INFORMATION IN THIS AFFIDAVIT IS WITHIN THE DEPONENT'S KNOWLEDGE AND IS TRUE. WHERE THE INFORMATION IS BASED ON ADVICE OR INFORMATION AND BELIEF, THIS IS STATED.

1. I am the witness to the signature of _____Jerry Stein_____ in this Renunciation of administration.

2. I was present and saw _____Jerry Stein_____ sign this document at _____Calgary_____, Alberta.

3. I know _____Jerry Stein_____ to be the person named in this Renunciation of administration.

4. I believe that _____Jerry Stein_____ is at least 18 years of age.

SWORN OR AFFIRMED BEFORE A COMMISSIONER FOR OATHS AT _____Calgary_____, ALBERTA ON _____October 2, 2011_____.

_____
Deponent

_____
Commissioner's Name

_____
Appointment Expiry Date

9. Fill in the date that the person signed the document.

10. The person making the nomination must sign on the signature line on the left hand side of the page, in front of a witness.

11. The witness must sign above the signature line on the right hand side of the page.

Form NC16 needs a Form NC11 attached. Follow the instructions for completing Form NC11 which was given in section **3.** of this chapter for Form NC15.

5. Form NC17 — Affidavit to Dispense with a Bond

Use NC17 if —

- you are the only administrator and you live outside of Alberta;

- there is more than one administrator, but none live in Alberta;

- you believe that a bond is not necessary to ensure that the administrator's work will be completed honestly and properly;

- you do not wish to post a bond;

- you have chosen "request to waive" on your Form NC1; and

- you are also filing a Form NC18.

Follow these steps to fill in Form NC17:

1. Fill in the estate name exactly as you did on the NC1.

2. Fill in the name of the person who will be swearing the affidavit (i.e., the deponent), who should be the administrator.

3. Fill in the date that the affidavit is sworn before a Commissioner for Oaths.

4. Do not change the sentence that appears in all capital letters.

5. In paragraph 2, describe how you are related to the deceased.

6. Do not change paragraphs 3 and 4. If you cannot swear under oath that both of those paragraphs are true, do not complete the NC17.

7. Fill in the name of the town or city where the document was signed and sworn. If there is more than one administrator, repeat the jurat (the line in all capitals just above the signature lines) and the signature line.

Sample 25
Form NC16

NC16

ESTATE NAME   William Brown, a.k.a. Bill Brown

DOCUMENT   **Nomination and consent to appointment of personal representative**

NAME   Dale Brown

COMPLETE ADDRESS   121 Second Street, Lethbridge, Alberta, T5T 5T5

1. The deceased, _____William Brown_____, signed a will in which _____Dale Brown_____ is appointed personal representative.

2. _____Dale Brown_____ has renounced all right and title to a grant of probate of the deceased's will.

   or

3. I have an interest in the administration of the deceased's estate because I am _____his son_____.

4. I nominate _____Sarah Brown_____ to apply for a grant of administration with will annexed of the deceased's property and consent to such an appointment.

SIGNED ON _____November 6, 2011_____.

_____Dale Brown_____   _____I.M. Witness_____
Signature   Witness

This document requires an affidavit of execution. Use Form NC11.

6. Form NC18 — Consent to Waive Bond

This document is not signed by the administrator; it is signed by the residuary beneficiaries of the estate. Each beneficiary must have his or her own Form NC18 to sign. You should prepare the documents for them, and once signed, the forms should be returned to you.

The purpose of the document is to tell the court that the beneficiaries of the estate are aware the administrator is applying to dispense with the bond and they feel secure in allowing the administrator to go ahead without it.

The document does not have to be sworn in front of a Commissioner for Oaths, but it does need to have a witness watch the beneficiary sign. The administrator should not be the witness on this form, though the beneficiaries can be witnesses for each other.

Follow these steps to fill in your Form NC18:

1. Fill in the estate name exactly as you did on Form NC1.

2. Fill in the name of the beneficiary.

3. Fill in the beneficiary's full address, including postal code.

4. There are two versions of paragraphs 1 and 2. You will have to choose the version that applies to your situation. Choose version one if there is a will and you are applying for administration with will annexed. Choose version two if there is no will and you are applying for administration. Delete the version that you are not using.

5. In paragraph 1, fill in the name of the deceased.

6. In paragraph 2, fill in the name of the person applying to be the administrator.

7. In paragraph 3, the person consenting to the waiver of the bond must describe how they are involved in the estate. For example, is the person a residuary beneficiary? A beneficiary on intestacy?

8. Do not change paragraph 4.

9. Fill in the date the document was signed by the beneficiary.

10. Have the beneficiary sign on the left hand side of the form on the line above "Signature."

11. Have a witness sign on the right hand side of the form.

12. The witness should clearly print his or her name below the signature.

Sample 26
Form NC17 (Administration)

NC17

ESTATE NAME — William Brown, a.k.a. Bill Brown

DOCUMENT — **Affidavit to dispense with a bond**

DEPONENT(S) NAME(S) — Sarah Brown

THE DEPONENT(S) EACH SWEAR UNDER OATH OR AFFIRM THAT THE INFORMATION IN THIS AFFIDAVIT IS WITHIN THE DEPONENTS' KNOWLEDGE AND IS TRUE. WHERE THE INFORMATION IS BASED ON ADVICE OR INFORMATION AND BELIEF, THIS IS STATED.

Applicant(s)

1. The applicant is entitled to apply for a grant because the applicant is the person with the highest priority to apply .

2. The applicant is fully familiar with the deceased's affairs because she is related to the deceased as _____ his daughter _____ .

Debts

3. The applicant has made a complete investigation of the deceased's affairs. To the best of our knowledge, Schedule 5 shows all the debts for which the deceased may be liable in the Province of Alberta and in any other jurisdiction.

4. The property of the estate is sufficient to pay all the debts shown in Schedule 5 and all the debts have been or will be paid before the distribution of the estate.

5. And therefore the applicant(s) request that this Court grant the application for a grant of _administration with will annexed_ without bond.

SWORN OR AFFIRMED BY EACH DEPONENT BEFORE A COMMISSIONER FOR OATHS AT _____ Lethbridge _____, ALBERTA ON _____ November 10, 2011 _____.

_____
Deponent

_____
Commissioner's Name

_____
Appointment Expiry Date

Form NC18 has a Form NC11 attached. Follow the instructions for the Form NC11 that are included above under the instructions for Form NC15 in section **3**.

7. Notices

7.1 Form NC19 — Notice to beneficaries (residuary)

With this form, you are letting each residuary beneficiary of the estate know about his or her entitlement under the estate. To determine which beneficiaries are the residuary beneficiaries, look for language such as "I leave the residue of my estate to … " or "I divide the rest of my estate equally among … " A homemade will might simply say "I leave my estate to … " Each beneficiary gets a separate notice, even if there is more than one beneficiary at the same address.

For instructions on completing Form NC19, see Chapter 12.

7.2 Form NC20 — Notice to beneficaries (non residuary)

Use Form NC20 if there is at least one person who is receiving a specific item (e.g., a ring, a vehicle) or specific sum of money (e.g., a gift of cash to a charity). This covers every beneficiary who is not receiving part of the residue. You will prepare a separate notice for each beneficiary. If a beneficiary is receiving a specific item as well as part of the residue, prepare both a Form NC20 and a Form NC19 for that person.

To fill in Form NC20, see Chapter 12.

7.3 Form NC22 — Notice to spouse of deceased: *Matrimonial Property Act*

Use Form NC22 if —

- the deceased was legally married (not common law) when he or she died, and

- the will does not leave 100 percent of the estate to the spouse.

Also use Form NC22 if —

- the deceased was legally married (not common law) when he or she died, and

- there is no will.

To fill in Form NC22, see Chapter 12.

Sample 27
Form NC18 (Administration)

NC18

ESTATE NAME	William Brown, a.k.a. Bill Brown
DOCUMENT	**Consent to waive bond**
NAME	June Brown
COMPLETE ADDRESS	612 Seventh Street, Edmonton, Alberta, T1T 1T1

1. The deceased, _____William Brown_____, died intestate.

2. _____Jerry Stein_____, who resides outside Alberta, is applying for a grant of administration.

3. I have an interest in the administration of the deceased's estate because I am _____his sister_____.

4. I understand that a bond is required because the applicant(s) reside outside Alberta. Nevertheless, I consent to an order of the court dispensing with any bond so required.

SIGNED ON _____November 10, 2011_____.

_____*June Brown*_____   _____*I.M. Witness*_____
Signature   Witness

This document must have Form NC11 attached.

7.4 Form NC23 — Notice to spouse/adult interdependent partner of deceased: *Dependants Relief Act*

Use NC23 if all of the following conditions apply —

- the deceased was legally married or had an adult interdependent partner at the time he or she died (see Chapter 12 for an explanation of adult interdependent partner);

- the spouse or adult interdependent partner resided in Canada at the time the deceased died; and

- the will does not leave 100 percent of the estate to the spouse or adult interdependent partner.

Also use NC23 if —

- the deceased was legally married or had an adult interdependent partner at the time he or she died;

- the spouse or adult interdependent partner resided in Canada at the time the deceased died; and

- there is no will.

To fill in Form NC23, see Chapter 12.

7.5 Form NC24.1 — Notice to the Public Trustee

Use NC24.1 if —

- there is a beneficiary of the estate who is not yet 18 years old;

- there is a beneficiary of the estate who is 18 or older now but was not yet 18 on the day the deceased died;

- the deceased left a biological or adopted child who is under the age of 18, even if the child is not named in the will;

- a beneficiary is missing (i.e. you know who it is but his or her whereabouts are unknown);

- the Public Trustee the court-appointed trustee for a beneficiary of the estate; or

- the Public Trustee is the attorney under an Enduring Power of Attorney for a beneficiary of the estate.

To fill in Form NC24.1, see Chapter 12.

7.6 Form NC25 — Affidavit regarding missing or unknown beneficiaries

Not many estates require Form NC25. It is intended to be used where there is difficulty identifying or finding a beneficiary, and the entire estate is being delayed while the executor searches for the person. Normally, the executor would keep searching and making enquiries, but if the executor has determined that the searches are pointless for now and the estate would be better off if the executor could get on with the rest of the estate administration, he or she would file this form.

As you will learn in this kit, beneficiaries of an estate must receive a written notice of their interest in the estate. If they cannot be identified or located, the executor is obviously not able to fulfill the requirement of serving the notice. The purpose of Form NC25 is to get the court's permission to go ahead without serving the person who cannot be identified or located. There are step-by-step instructions for completing Form NC25 in Chapter 6.

11

Compiling and Filing Your Application

1. Put Documents in Order

Now that you have prepared all of the individual documents that together make up an application for probate or administration, you must put them together properly so that the bundle of documents (known collectively as "the application") can be filed with the Clerk of the Court of Queen's Bench (Surrogate). The Surrogate Court is a division of the Court of Queen's Bench of Alberta that deals with probate matters.

The documents are put together in one bundle held together with a staple or clip. To put them in the right order, follow the "NC" numbering at the top right hand corner of the documents. Start with NC1 on top, and include each document you have prepared. If you are not using any particular document, simply leave it out. Do not include a blank document. It is okay if you skip from, say, NC19 to NC27, if the circumstances of the estate are such that you do not need the documents in between.

When you prepared your NC1, you also prepared a backer. Put this behind all of your other documents, but place it so that the blank side of the sheet is facing up and the side with wording is facing out. This means that the backer will act as a back cover for your application, much like the back cover of a book.

2. Where to Sign

There are several places for you to sign your application. Check over your documents to ensure that you have not missed any. They are:

- Form NC1
- Form NC2 (sworn)
- Forms NC19, NC20, and NC21, depending on which are included in your particular application
- Form NC22
- Form NC23
- Form NC27 (sworn)
- Back of original will (In Chapter 4, section **3.**, there are instructions for adding words to the back of the last page of the will which must be signed. The wording of the sample must be followed.)

3. Find a Commissioner for Oaths

You will note that two of the documents in the list above must be sworn in front of a Commissioner for Oaths. These documents do not need to be notarized by a Notary Public unless you are signing them outside of Alberta. Chapter 4, section **6.** lists some suggestions of where you might find a Commissioner for Oaths who can help you. Note that some charge a fee and some do not.

4. Make Copies

Before taking your documents to the courts for filing, make one photocopy of everything you are filing. Photocopy the back of the will with its stamps and signatures as well. Take the original and the copy with you when you go to file your documents. The Clerk of the Court will stamp your photocopied application and write a court file number on it. Once you have the stamp and file number, make several more photocopies of the entire bundle. You will need one copy for each residuary beneficiary of the estate. If you are serving your application on the Office of the Public Trustee, you will need one for them as well. Each spouse or former spouse of the deceased who receives a notice will also need a copy of the application.

5. How, When, and Where to File Documents

Filing of your documents is done at the courthouse in the judicial district that you named in the documents. Do not send the documents by mail, courier, or email, and do not fax them in. Take them in person or have someone do it for you in person.

You will give the documents to a Clerk of the Surrogate Court, which is a part of the Court of Queen's Bench of Alberta. In Calgary and Edmonton, there is a separate counter where clerks deal only with Surrogate matters. In all other centres, there is no separate counter for Surrogate matters, so you will file your documents directly with the Queen's Bench clerk.

Filing means that you give the originals and one copy of everything to the clerk. He or she will do a quick review of your documents to make sure that you signed everything, swore them in front of a Commissioner for Oaths, and that all necessary pages and parts are attached. If all appears to be fine, the clerk will keep the originals and stamp them with a court file number. He or she will also stamp that number onto the copy of the application and give you back the copy.

You will pay the court fee at this time. For help determining what your court fee will be, see section **6.** in this chapter.

The clerk will give the documents a much closer look later on to make sure all details are correct and in the right places. If everything in your documentation is acceptable, the clerk will give your application to a justice (judge) of the Court of Queen's Bench. The judge will also review your application. If everything is fine, the judge will sign it, which means you will soon get your Grant of Probate or Grant of Administration in the mail.

If your documents are not acceptable, the clerk will mail them back to you and ask you to correct them and bring them back again. Note that if you do not make the corrections, the judge will never see your application. The clerk will include a checklist and perhaps some notes about what needs to be corrected. There may be more than one problem with your documents. If you do not understand what you are being asked to do, telephone the clerk or take your documents to the clerk and ask for specific details. They are used to people doing their own applications and will help you if you need it.

The following is a list of addresses and phone numbers for the Clerks of the Court of Queen's Bench across Alberta (Surrogate Court in Calgary and Edmonton):

Calgary Courts Centre
601 – 5th Street SW T2P 5P7
Suite 705 - N
(403) 297-7538

Drumheller Court House
511 – 3 Avenue West, PO Box 759 T0J 0Y0
(403) 820-7300

Edmonton Law Courts Building,
1A Sir Winston Churchill Square T5J 0R2
(780) 422-2492

Fort McMurray Court House,
9700 Franklin Avenue T9H 4W3
(780) 743-7195

Grande Prairie Court House
10260 – 99 Street T8V 2H4
(780) 538-5340

High Level Court House
10106 – 100 Avenue, PO Box 1560 T0H 1Z0
(780) 926-3715

Hinton Court House
237 Jasper Street West, PO Box 6450 T7V 1X7
(780) 865-8280

Lethbridge Court House
320 – 4 Street South T1J 1Z8
(403) 381-5196

Medicine Hat Law Courts
460 – 1 Street SE T1A 0A8
(403) 529-8710

Peace River Court House
9905 – 97 Avenue, Bag 900-34 T8S 1T4
(780) 624-6256

Red Deer Court House,
4909 – 48 Avenue T4N 3T5
(403) 340-5220

St. Paul Court House
4704 – 50 Street, PO Box 1900 T0A 3A0
(780) 645-6324

Wetaskiwin Law Courts
4605 – 51 Street T9A 1K7
(780) 361-1258

6. Court Fees

To determine how much your court fee will be, look for the net value figure at the bottom of the last page of your NC7 Inventory. Your fee is based on the net value. Find where that net value figure falls in the chart of court fees found in Chapter 2, section **4**. This will tell you how much you must pay.

In most places, the Clerk of the Court will ask you for payment at the time you file your documents. In other places, they will ask for the payment when you pick up your processed Grant of Probate or Grant of Administration.

You can pay using cash, debit, Visa, or MasterCard.

12

Notices to Beneficiaries and Spouses

In every estate, whether you are applying for probate or administration, you will have to send out at least one notice. The purpose of the various notices is to let the people involved know of their rights under the will. Serving these notices is a requirement under the Surrogate Rules, and you will not get your Grant of Probate or Grant of Administration if you do not serve the notices.

As every individual has different family members and friends around him or her, and a different will, you will have to decide who needs to receive a notice. The people who must receive notices fall into two general groups. One group is made up of the beneficiaries, who are the people who will be inheriting something from the estate. This group includes —

- beneficiaries receiving all or some of the residue of the estate under a will;
- beneficiaries receiving a specific item or gift from the estate under a will; and
- beneficiaries on intestacy (i.e., where there is no will).

The other group includes legally married spouses, common-law spouses, and adult interdependent partners. Unlike the beneficiary group, the people in the spousal group only get notices if they are receiving anything less than the entire estate. Note that some people may fall into both groups, which means they will get more than one notice.

The notices are usually prepared after you have created all of the required and specialized documents so that you already have all of the information at hand about who is to be sent a notice. If you have prepared those documents already, making up your notices should be a fairly quick process. Look at your Form NC6 (described in Chapter 9) to see who is named as a beneficiary and who is listed as a spouse.

You may not need to use every notice that is provided in this kit. Just choose the ones that apply to your situation. Each notice is described in this chapter and notes are included to help you decide whether or not you need that notice. If a person is receiving two or three notices, each of which requires you to send a copy of the application, send all of the notices together with one copy of the application. If a person is receiving two notices, one that requires you to send a copy of the application and one that does not, send the notices together with one copy of the application.

1. How to Use the Acknowledgement Section (Where Applicable)

You will notice that most of the notices have a section at the bottom of the page in all capital letters. This part of the document is called the Acknowledgement. It provides a place for the person receiving the notice (i.e., the spouse or the beneficiary) to acknowledge in writing that he or she has received it.

If you send a notice to someone who refuses to sign and return it, this will not hurt your application to the court. You are not required to get agreement or cooperation. The Form NC27 Affidavit of service will show that you have given them their notices in the proper way; this fulfills your requirements.

The acknowledgement can be extremely useful when the executor of the estate is a beneficiary or spouse of the deceased. Without the acknowledgement, if you are the executor or administrator as well as a beneficiary or spouse, you would have to send yourself a registered letter with a notice in it. To avoid that silly situation, you may create the notice and sign the acknowledgement section right away to show that you received your notice.

If you sign the acknowledgement on your own notice, take the following steps with your own notice only:

1. Do not put your notice in Form NC27 with the other notices; and

2. Put your original signed notice in your application for probate or administration, after all of the other documents.

Taking these steps has the same legal effect as sending yourself registered mail and then filing an affidavit (as described in Chapter 5 and this chapter under Form NC27) to prove it, but this way is quicker, easier, and makes more sense.

2. Form NC19 — Notice to Beneficiaries (Residuary)

Every Application for Probate must have at least one residuary beneficiary. There could be more if the will dictates it. An Application for Administration will only have a residuary beneficiary if it is an Application for Administration with Will Annexed. If you are applying for administration but not with will annexed, you do not need this form.

Use Form NC19 for an Application for Probate if —

- there is only one person getting the whole estate;
- the will uses words such as "the residue of my estate" or "the rest of my property"; or
- the will uses words like "divide my estate among my children," in which the estate is given to a group of people.

Use Form NC19 for an Application for Administration with Will Annexed if —

- there is only one person getting the whole estate;
- the will uses words such as "the residue of my estate" or "the rest of my property"; or
- the will uses words like "divide my estate among my children," in which the estate is given to a group of people.

Use the following steps to prepare your Form NC19 (shown in Sample 28):

1. Fill in the name of the deceased exactly as you did on Form NC1.

2. Beside "To:" fill in the name of the beneficiary as it appears in the will. Sometimes names have changed, such as when a married woman takes her husband's name. In this situation, fill in the name that the beneficiary currently uses, followed by the words "in the will described as ... " and the name as it shows in the will. For example, Mr. Smith dies, leaving his estate to his daughter Mary Ann Smith. After the will was made, Mary Ann married Mr. Wilson. The Form NC19 for Mary Ann would be to "Mary Ann Wilson, in the will described as Mary Ann Smith."

3. Fill in the beneficiary's full street address and mailing address, including postal code.

4. In the next line, fill in the name of the deceased as it appears at the top of the page.

5. Under "The will gives you," fill in the gift that the beneficiary is entitled to receive. This is always a percentage (e.g., 50 percent) or fraction (e.g., ½) of the residue of the estate. If it is the whole estate, simply say "100 percent of the estate."

6. At the end of the next sentence, insert either "probate" or "administration with will annexed."

7. Do not change the next two paragraphs.

8. In the last line of the document, fill in your name, address, and telephone number.

9. At the bottom of the document, sign on the line on the left hand side and fill in the date on the line on the right hand side. Fill in your name and address, including postal code, below your signature.

10. If you are the person receiving the notice, sign and date the acknowledgement section.

Note that everyone who gets a Form NC19 also gets a full copy of the entire application, including the will.

3. Form NC20 — Notice to Beneficiaries (Non Residuary)

Use Form NC20 if —

- you are applying for a grant of probate or administration with will annexed; and

- there is somebody named in the will to receive a specific gift such as a piece of jewelry, a vehicle, household goods, or a specific sum of cash (this includes a gift to a charity).

There may be individuals who will receive a specific gift as well as a share of the residue. This means that you will prepare both a Form NC19 for the residue and a Form NC20 for the specific item.

Use the following steps to prepare your Form NC20 (as shown in Sample 29):

Sample 28
Form NC19

ESTATE NAME   Samuel Winston France, a.k.a. Sammy France

DOCUMENT   **Notice to beneficiaries (residuary)**

To: Name: Sarah France

       Complete address: 22 Robson Street

                     Vancouver, B.C.

                     V7V 7V7

You are named as a residuary beneficiary in the last will of ___Samuel Winston France___.

The will gives you ___50 percent of the estate___.

The personal representative(s) named in the will have applied for a grant of ___probate___. Enclosed with this notice is a copy of the application for a grant of ___probate___. This includes a copy of the will and a list of the estate property and debts.

Once the court issues the grant, the personal representative(s) will collect in the property, pay the debts, and complete the administration of the estate and anything else required of the personal representative(s). Then they will be in a position to account to you before distributing any estate left after payment of all debts and expenses.

By issuing the grant, the court is not approving the figures submitted in the application for a grant of ___probate___. It is the responsibility of the beneficiary(ies) to supervise the actions of the personal representative(s).

You can contact ___Lillian France___ at ___4550 – 450 Avenue, Edmonton, Alberta, T5T 5T5___, phone ___780-555-5555___, for any further information you may need.

Lillian France
_____
Personal Representative

October 1, 2011
_____
Date

Name: Lillian France

Complete address: 4550 – 450 Avenue

                  Edmonton, Alberta

                  T5T 5T5

I ACKNOWLEDGE RECEIPT OF THIS NOTICE AND OF A COPY OF THE APPLICATION FOR A GRANT OF ___PROBATE___ **IN THE ESTATE OF** ___SAMUEL WINSTON FRANCE___.

Lillian France
_____
Beneficiary

October 1, 2011
_____
Date

1. Fill in the name of the deceased exactly as you did on Form NC1.

2. Beside "To:" fill in the name of the beneficiary as it appears in the will. Sometimes names have changed, such as when a married woman takes her husband's name. In this situation, fill in the name that the beneficiary currently uses, followed by the words "in the will described as ... " and then the name as it shows in the will. For example, Mr. Smith dies, leaving his estate to his daughter Mary Ann Smith. After the will was made, Mary Ann married Mr. Wilson. The Form NC19 for Mary Ann would be to "Mary Ann Wilson, in the will described as Mary Ann Smith."

3. Fill in the beneficiary's full street address and mailing address, including postal code.

4. In the next line, fill in the name of the deceased as it appears at the top of the page.

5. Under "The will gives you," fill in the gift that the beneficiary is entitled to receive. Use the wording in the will if possible, or match it as closely as possible.

6. At the end of the next sentence, insert either "probate" or "administration with will annexed."

7. Do not change the next paragraph.

8. In the last line of the document, fill in your name, address, and telephone number.

9. At the bottom of the document, sign on the line on the left hand side and fill in the date on the line on the right hand side. Fill in your name and address, including postal code, below your signature.

10. If you are the person receiving the notice, sign and date the acknowledgement section.

11. Do not send the beneficiaries who receive a Form NC20 a full copy of the entire application or the whole will.

4. Form NC21 — Notice to Beneficiaries (Intestacy)

Form NC21 is designed to notify beneficiaries who will inherit something when the deceased did not leave a will. Refer to the chart in section **7.** in Chapter 8 to see who should inherit in your situation. This information will also be set out in the Form NC6 schedule of beneficiaries. Each beneficiary gets his or her own notice.

Sample 29
Form NC20

NC20

ESTATE NAME   Samuel Winston France, a.k.a. Sammy France

DOCUMENT   **Notice to beneficiaries (non residuary)**

To: Name: _Lillian France_

Complete address: _4550 – 450 Avenue_
Edmonton, Alberta
_T5T 5T5_

You are named as a non-residuary beneficiary in the last will of _____.

The will gives you _____.

The personal representative(s) named in the will have applied for a grant of ___probate___
_____.

Once the court issues the grant, the personal representative(s) will collect in the estate property, pay the debts, and complete the administration of the estate and anything else required of the personal representative(s). Then they will be in a position to distribute your gift to you as long as it is not needed to pay for debts and expenses of the estate.

You can contact _____Lillian France_____ at __4550 – 450 Avenue, Edmonton, Alberta,__
__T5T 5T5__, phone _____780-555-5555_____, for any further information you may need.

Lillian France   _October 1, 2011_
Personal Representative   Date

Name: _Lillian France_
Complete address: _4550 – 450 Avenue_
Edmonton, Alberta
_T5T 5T5_

I ACKNOWLEDGE RECEIPT OF THIS NOTICE AND OF A COPY OF THE APPLICATION FOR A GRANT OF _____PROBATE_____ **IN THE ESTATE OF** ___SAMUEL WINSTON FRANCE___.

Lillian France   _October 1, 2011_
Beneficiary   **Date**

Use Form NC21 if —

- there is no will; and

- you are applying for administration.

Use the following steps to prepare Form NC21:

2. Beside"To:" fill in the name of the beneficiary as it appears in the will. Sometimes names have changed, such as when a married woman takes her husband's name. In this situation, fill in the name that the beneficiary currently uses, followed by the words "in the will described as … " and then fill in the name as it shows in the will. For example, Mr. Smith dies, leaving his estate to his daughter Mary Ann Smith. After the will was made, Mary Ann married Mr. Wilson. The Form NC19 for Mary Ann would be to "Mary Ann Wilson, in the will described as Mary Ann Smith."

3. Fill in the beneficiary's full name, street address, and mailing address, including postal code.

4. In the next line, fill in the name of the deceased as it appears at the top of the page.

5. Under "you will receive," fill in the gift that the beneficiary is entitled to receive. This will usually be expressed as a percentage (e.g., "50 percent of the estate") or a fraction (e.g., "half of the estate").

6. Fill in your name as the person applying for a grant of administration.

7. Do not change the next three paragraphs.

8. In the last line of the document, fill in your name, address, and telephone number.

9. At the bottom of the document, sign on the line on the left hand side and fill in the date on the right hand side. Fill in your name and address, including postal code, below your signature.

10. If you are the person receiving the notice, sign and date the acknowledgement section.

Each of the beneficiaries who receives a Form NC21 must also receive a full copy of the entire application for administration, including the will.

5. Form NC22 — Notice to Spouse of Deceased: *Matrimonial Property Act*

Use Form NC22 if —

- the deceased was legally married (not common law) at the time he or she passed away, and

- the spouse is not receiving the entire estate.

Also use Form NC22 if —

- the deceased was divorced within the last two years prior to his or her death, and

- the former spouse is not receiving the entire estate.

Use the following steps to prepare your Form NC22:

1. Fill in the name of the deceased exactly as you did on Form NC1.

2. Beside "To:" fill in the name of the beneficiary as it appears in the will if there is a will. Sometimes names have changed, such as when a married woman takes her husband's name. In this situation, fill in the name that the beneficiary currently uses, followed by the words "in the will described as..." and then the name as it shows in the will. For example, Mr. Smith dies, leaving his estate to his wife Jane Smith. After the will was made, Jane married Mr. Wilson. The Form NC19 for Jane would be to "Jane Wilson, in the will described as Jane Smith."

3. Fill in the beneficiary's full street address and mailing address, including postal code.

4. In the next line, select either "probate," "administration," or "administration with will annexed."

5. Do not change the next four paragraphs.

6. Sign on the signature line above "Personal Representative" on the left hand side, and fill in the date on the right hand side. Fill in your name and address, including postal code, below your signature.

7. If you are the person receiving the notice, sign and date the acknowledgement section.

Each of the beneficiaries who receives a Form NC21 must also receive a full copy of the entire application, including the will.

Sample 30
Form NC21

NC21

ESTATE NAME   Samuel Winston France, a.k.a. Sammy France

DOCUMENT   **Notice to beneficiaries (intestacy)**

To: Name: Jeremy Smith
         Complete address: 222 44th Street
                           Edmonton, Alberta T2T 2T2

Samuel Winston France died without leaving a will. In this circumstance, the provisions of the *Intestate Succession Act* of Alberta determine which relatives of the deceased inherit the estate.

You are one of these relatives, or beneficiary (intestacy), and you will receive 25 percent of the estate.

Lillian France has applied for a grant of administration.

Enclosed with this notice is a copy of the application for a grant of administration. This includes a list of the property and debts.

Once the court issues the grant, the personal representative(s) will collect in the property, pay the debts, and complete the administration of the estate and anything else required of the personal representative(s). Then they will be in a position to account to you before distributing any estate left after payment of all debts and expenses.

By issuing the grant, the court is not approving the figures submitted in the application for a grant of administration. It is the responsibility of the beneficiary(ies) to supervise the actions of the personal representative(s).

You can contact Lillian France at 4550 – 450 Avenue, Edmonton, Alberta, T5T 5T5, phone 780-555-5555, for any further information you may need.

_____   _Lillian France_
Lillian France   October 1, 2011
Personal Representative   Date

Name: Lillian France
Complete address: 4550 – 450 Avenue
                          Edmonton, Alberta T5T 5T5

I ACKNOWLEDGE RECEIPT OF THIS NOTICE AND OF A COPY OF THE APPLICATION FOR A GRANT OF ADMINISTRATION IN THE ESTATE OF SAMUEL WINSTON FRANCE.

_____   _____
Beneficiary   **Date**

6. Form NC23 — Notice to Spouse/Adult Interdependent Partner of Deceased: *Dependants Relief Act*

Use Form NC23 if all of the following apply —

- there is a valid will that you are using to apply for probate or for administration with will annexed;

- the deceased, at the time he or she died, had a spouse or a common law spouse; and

- the spouse or common law spouse is not receiving the entire estate under the will.

Also use form NC23 if —

- there is no will; and

- the spouse or common-law spouse is inheriting some of the estate (but not all of it) on intestacy.

Use the following steps to prepare Form NC23:

1. Fill in the name of the deceased exactly as you did on Form NC1.

2. Beside "To:" fill in the name of the beneficiary as it appears in the will. Sometimes names have changed, such as when a married woman takes her husband's name. In this situation, fill in the name that the beneficiary currently uses, followed by the words "in the will described as ... " and then the name as it shows in the will.

3. Fill in the beneficiary's full street address and mailing address, including postal code.

4. In the next line, insert either "probate," "administration," or "administration with will annexed."

5. In the next line, fill in the name of the deceased.

6. Do not change the next three paragraphs.

7. At the bottom of the document, sign on the line on the left hand side and fill in the date on the line on the right hand side. Fill in your name and address, including postal code, below your signature.

8. If you are the person receiving the notice, sign and date the acknowledgement section.

Each of the beneficiaries who receives a Form NC23 must also receive a full copy of the entire application, including the will.

Sample 31
Form NC22

NC22

ESTATE NAME	Samuel Winston France, a.k.a. Sammy France
DOCUMENT	**Notice to spouse of deceased**
	Matrimonial Property Act

To: Name: Carolann France

Complete address: 1224 South Street

Calgary, Alberta T2T 2T2

Enclosed with this notice is a copy of the application for a grant of
administration .

The *Matrimonial Property Act* gives rights to a spouse or former spouse in certain circumstances and the law requires that the notice be given to you because you are the spouse or a former spouse and have not been given all of the property in the estate.

You may have a claim under the *Matrimonial Property Act* on the property in the estate. This must be dealt with before the estate can be finally distributed.

There are some time requirements that must be met. You must begin any application before the expiration of six months from the date the court issued the grant of probate or administration. There are other time limits in the Act which may mean that in your case you have less than six months in which to act, after that, the personal representative may distribute the property.

If you want to take this further, you must consult your own lawyer immediately.

Lillian France
_____   _____
Personal Representative   October 1, 2011
                                                          Date

Name: Lillian France

Complete address: 4550 – 450 Avenue

Edmonton, Alberta T5T 5T5

I ACKNOWLEDGE RECEIPT OF THIS NOTICE AND OF A COPY OF THE APPLICATION FOR A GRANT OF ___ADMINISTRATION___ **IN THE ESTATE OF** SAMUEL WINSTON FRANCE.

_____   _____
              Spouse   **Date**

7. Form NC24 — Notice to a Dependent Child of the Deceased: *Dependants Relief Act*

Use Form NC24 if —

- you are applying for a grant of administration and the deceased left a minor child by blood or adoption; or

- the deceased left an adult child who cannot earn a living due to a handicap.

Also use Form NC24 if —

- you are applying for a grant of probate or administration with will annexed, and the deceased left a minor child by blood or adoption; or

- the deceased left an adult child who cannot earn a living due to a handicap, and the deceased did not leave the full estate to the child in the will.

The NC24 document should be addressed to the trustee of the dependent child. If it is an adult handicapped child, there may be a trustee who was appointed by the court. If it is a minor child, the document can be addressed to the surviving parent of the child.

Use the following steps to prepare your Form NC24:

1. Fill in the name of the deceased exactly as you did on Form NC1.

2. Beside "To:" fill in the name of the trustee of the beneficiary.

3. Fill in the trustee's full street address and mailing address, including postal code.

4. Fill in the name of the minor child or adult handicapped person.

5. In the next line, insert either "probate," "administration," or "administration with will annexed."

6. In the next line, fill in the name of the deceased.

7. Do not change the next three paragraphs.

8. At the bottom of the document, sign on the line on the left hand side and fill in the date on the line on the right hand side. Fill in your name and address, including postal code, below your signature.

9. If you are the person receiving the notice, sign and date the acknowledgement section.

Sample 32
Form NC23

NC23

ESTATE NAME   Samuel Winston France, a.k.a. Sammy France

DOCUMENT   **Notice to spouse or adult interdependent partner of deceased**
Dependants Relief Act

To: Name: Carolann France
       Complete address: 1224 South Street
                      Calgary, Alberta T2T 2T2

Enclosed with this notice is a copy of the application for a grant of
           probate   .

The law requires that this notice must be given to you because you are the spouse or adult interdependent partner of   Samuel Winston France   but you have not been given all the property in the estate.

The *Dependants Relief Act* gives rights to a spouse or adult interdependent partner that allow the spouse or adult interdependent partner to apply to the court to receive more or all of the estate. The court can change the distribution of the estate and give you more if the court decides the circumstances warrant it.

There are some time requirements which must be met before the court can hear any application. You should begin your application before six months have gone by from the date the court issued the grant of probate or administration. After that, the personal representative may distribute the estate property and you can only apply if the court lets you. You can then only ask for some or all of the property in the estate that is still undistributed at that time.

If you want to take this further, you must consult your own lawyer immediately.

Lillian France   October 1, 2011
Personal Representative   Date

Name: Lillian France
Complete address: 4550 – 450 Avenue
                   Edmonton, Alberta T5T 5T5

I ACKNOWLEDGE RECEIPT OF THIS NOTICE AND OF A COPY OF THE APPLICATION FOR A GRANT OF   PROBATE   **IN THE ESTATE OF**   SAMUEL WINSTON FRANCE   .

_____   _____
Spouse or Adult Interdependent Partner   **Date**

Sample 33
Form NC24

NC24

ESTATE NAME   Samuel Winston France, a.k.a. Sammy France

DOCUMENT   **Notice to a dependent child of the deceased**
Dependants Relief Act

To: Name of Trustee: <u>I.M. Trustee</u>

   Complete address: <u>622 Parkview Road</u>
           <u>Edmonton, Alberta T1T 1T1</u>

   On behalf of the dependent child: <u>Jane France</u> .

Enclosed with this notice is a copy of the application for a grant of
<u> administration </u>.

The law requires that this notice must be given to you because you may be a dependent
child of <u> Samuel Winstron France </u> but you have not been given all the property in the
estate.

The *Dependants Relief Act* gives rights to a dependent child that allow the dependent
child to apply to the court to receive more or all of the estate. The court can change the
distribution of the estate and give you more if the court decides you are a dependent and
the circumstances warrant it.

There are some time requirements which must be met before the court can hear any
application. You should begin your application before six months have gone by from the
date the court issued the grant of <u> administration </u>. After that, the personal
                 probate or administration
representative may distribute the estate property and you can only apply if the court lets
you. You can then only ask for some or all of the property in the estate that is still
undistributed at that time.

If you want to take this further, you must consult your own lawyer immediately.

<u> Lillian France </u>   <u> October 1, 2011 </u>
  Personal Representative   Date

Name: <u>Lillian France</u>
Complete address: <u>4550 – 450 Avenue</u>
       <u>Edmonton, Alberta T5T 5T5</u>

**I ACKNOWLEDGE RECEIPT OF THIS NOTICE AND OF A COPY OF THE
APPLICATION FOR A GRANT OF** <u> ADMINISTRATION </u> **IN THE ESTATE
OF** <u> SAMUEL WINSTON FRANCE </u>.

<u>   </u>   <u>   </u>
   Trustee   Date

Each of the beneficiaries who receives a Form NC24 must also receive a full copy of the entire application, including the will.

8. Are Common-Law Spouses Supposed to Be Served with Notices?

In Alberta, common-law spouses are called adult interdependent partners, explained in more detail in section **9.** If there is an adult interdependent partner involved in the estate you are administering, you will serve him or her with an NC23 because he or she has the same right to inherit as a legally married spouse. However, you do not serve an NC22 on a common-law spouse, because that notice, as indicated above, has to do with divorce between legally married people only.

9. What Are Adult Interdependent Partners?

This term refers to a person who lives in an adult interdependent relationship. This legal concept is unique to Alberta, and includes common-law opposite-sex couples and common-law same-sex couples. A person is an adult interdependent partner of the deceased if that person meets all of these requirements —

- is an adult,
- was not legally married to the deceased,
- lived in a relationship of interdependence with the deceased (a relationship of interdependence does not necessarily include a sexual relationship. The determining factors are that the deceased and this person shared their lives, were emotionally connected, and functioned as an economic and domestic unit),
- lived with the deceased for at least three years (or less if they had a child together),
- was not related to the deceased by blood, and
- was not providing domestic support or personal care (e.g., nanny, housekeeper, caregiver for aging person) for money or for other consideration.

There can only be one adult interdependent partner at a time. It is, however, possible to have both a legally married spouse and an adult interdependent partner at the same time.

10. How and When to Serve the Notices

Once you have prepared the notices that you need and have signed them as executor, make three photocopies of each one that you are going to send out to (serve on) beneficiaries or spouses. A sample letter for serving notices is included on the CD-ROM.

It is essential that you do not mail out original notices to the beneficiaries. You must keep the original signed notices for your Form NC27 Affidavit of service. For each beneficiary or spouse, make up a package that includes:

- Two photocopies of the notice (Remember that a person may be entitled to different notices as discussed above. In that case, include two photocopies of each notice.)

- A photocopy of the entire application for probate, administration, or administration with will annexed, as follows —

  - include each individual document (Form NC1 through NC18) you created for anyone receiving NC20, NC21, NC22, NC23, NC24, or NC25,

  - include the will (if applicable),

  - do not include any notices to beneficiaries other than the individual who is getting the package, and

  - do not send the Form NC1 through NC18 documents to a person who is receiving a Form NC19 notice and no other notice.

All notices must be sent by registered mail by the executor. When you send the notices out, keep the post office receipts for your Form NC27 Affidavit of service.

Put the original signed notices and the post office receipts aside to be used in the preparation of your Form NC27.

11. Serving the Public Trustee

You must serve a notice on the Office of the Public Trustee only if one of the following applies:

- any beneficiary of the estate was a minor on the day the deceased died;

- the deceased left behind a minor child who is not inheriting anything under the estate;

- one of the beneficiaries is a person who has been declared a missing person by the courts; or

- one of the beneficiaries is a handicapped or elderly adult for whom the Public Trustee acts as trustee.

Do not make the mistake, as many executors do, of assuming that you do not have to serve the Public Trustee if a minor child in the estate still has a living parent, or if the minor child is not named as a beneficiary of the estate. Even where that is the case, you still have to serve the notice. The Public Trustee's job in an estate like that is to look out for the welfare of the minor child.

There are two Offices of the Public Trustee in Alberta. Pick the one that is geographically closest to the deceased's usual place of residence. They are:

- Calgary:
  2100 Telus Tower
  411 – 1st Street SE
  Calgary, AB T2G 4Y5
  403-297-6541 (310-0000, toll-free in Alberta)

- Edmonton:
  103 4th Floor
  J.E. Brownlee Building
  10365 – 97 Street T5J 3Z8
  780-427-2744 (310-0000, toll-free in Alberta)

The form that you will use to give notice to the Public Trustee, no matter which particular situation requires you to give the notice, is called Form NC24.1 (see Sample 31). Instructions for completing this form are below. This notice is very unlike any of the other notices you have completed so far. You will see that the notice has two pages. You must complete the first page but not the second, although you will send both pages. The Public Trustee will complete the second page after you have served it on them.

Use the following steps to prepare Form NC24.1:

1. Fill in the name of the deceased exactly as you did on Form NC1.

2. In the first paragraph, insert either "probate," "administration," or "administration with will annexed."

3. You will have to check off the appropriate boxes. The boxes under 1 refer to individuals who are named in a will or are beneficiaries on intestacy. The boxes under 2 refer to individuals who are dependants of the deceased (they may be the same as 1 or may be different).

4. For each box that you check off, fill in the required name, date of birth, and address of the beneficiary or dependant. Note that if there is more than one person under any checked box, you should include the name, date of birth, and address for each one, even if that makes your document longer than a page.

5. Sign on the line on the bottom, left-hand side and fill in the date.

6. Do not fill in anything or cross off anything below the words "To the Court of Queen's Bench of Alberta ... "

As with other notices, make several photocopies. Send by registered mail one photocopy of the notice together with a copy of the will (if applicable) and all of the documents from Form NC1 through NC18.

12. Preparing Your Affidavit of Service

The Affidavit of service is a document that you will use to describe to the court the following:

- Which notices you prepared
- To whom you sent the notices
- To what addresses you sent the notices
- When you sent the notices
- How you sent the notices

The fact that it is an affidavit means that you must swear its contents to be true in front of a Commissioner for Oaths. Once it is sworn, you will file it at the court at the same time as your application for probate or administration (see Chapter 11 about compiling and filing your documents), and your affidavit becomes written court evidence. You do not need a separate Form NC27 for each beneficiary; in fact, you may be able to prepare just one that includes all beneficiaries and spouses in the estate.

The Affidavit of service is Form NC27, regardless of whether you are applying for probate, administration, or administration with will annexed. Because this document is both complicated and essential, there is a sample completed Form NC27 included in this kit for you to use as a guide, in addition to the blank form. See Sample 35.

Use the following steps to prepare your Form NC27:

1. Fill in the court file number from your Form NC1.

2. Fill in the name of the deceased exactly as you did on Form NC1.

Sample 34
Form NC24.1

NC24.1

ESTATE NAME   Samuel Winston France, a.k.a. Sammy France

DOCUMENT   **Notice to the Public Trustee**

This gives you notice that the personal representative shown in the attached copy of an Application for a grant of _____probate_____ has applied for this grant.

Notice is given to you

1. under section 6 of the *Administration of Estates Act* (beneficiaries interested in the estate)

    [   ] A minor at the date of death of the deceased
           Name:
           Date of Birth:
           Address:
    [   ] A person who has been declared to be a missing person by an Order of the Court
           Name:
           Address:
    [   ] A represented adult for whose estate you are trustee
           Name:
           Address:

2. under section 7 of the *Administration of Estates Act* (dependants)

    [X] The deceased was survived by a minor child of the deceased
           Name: Jessica France
           Date of Birth: August 1, 2008
           Address: 999 First Street, Edmonton, Alberta, T1T 1T2
    [   ] The deceased was survived by a represented adult child for whose estate you are trustee
           Name:
           Address:

Lillian France
Personal Representative

_____August 1, 2011_____
Date

Name: Office of the Public Trustee

Sample 34 — Continued

To the Court of Queen's Bench of Alberta and the personal representative:

The Public Trustee

   [ ] does not intend to be represented on this application
   [ ] intends to be represented on this application

The Public Trustee confirms the following:

   [ ] Any property to which a minor child is entitled from the estate must be delivered to the Public Trustee.

   [ ] Clause _____ of the will appoints _____ as trustee of money or property to which the minor(s) _____ is (are) entitled under the will. The will does not appoint the Public Trustee to monitor on behalf of the minor(s). Accordingly, the Public Trustee will not monitor the trustee on behalf of the minor(s) unless the Court directs the Public Trustee to monitor pursuant to section 22 of the *Public Trustee Act*.

   [ ] Clause _____ of the will appoints _____ as trustee of money or property to which the minor(s) _____ is (are) entitled under the will and clause _____ appoints the Public Trustee to monitor on behalf of the minor(s). Accordingly, the Public Trustee will monitor the trustee on behalf of the minor(s).

   [ ] The Public Trustee reserves the right to apply under the provisions of the *Dependants Relief Act* on behalf of _____.

_____   _____
    Public Trustee of Alberta   Date

The Court of Queen's Bench requires submissions to be made as to whether the Public Trustee should monitor the trust for the benefit of minor beneficiaries. Either the applicant or the Public Trustee, on notice to the other, must arrange for the Court to hear the submissions.

_____   _____
    Justice of the Court of Queen's Bench   Date

3. Fill in the deponent's name. The deponent is the person who is swearing the affidavit, so it will be the person who mailed or delivered the documents. This is almost always the executor or administrator.

4. Do not change the paragraph below the solid line that appears in all capital letters.

5. In the first blank, put in the date that you mailed or delivered your documents to the beneficiaries and/or spouses. If there is more than one date, you will have to repeat the contents of the Form NC27 for that date.

6. The documents that you served on a beneficiary or spouse have to be listed, starting at A. For example, A would be your Form NC1 Application, B would be NC2 Affidavit, and so forth. List notices here as well.

7. Photocopy each document that is listed.

8. Next to "on the following," list the people to whom you mailed or delivered a package of documents. Include names and addresses.

9. Below the list of names and addresses, describe how you served the documents. Some choices are:

   - *(for notices)* I served these documents by sending each person named above a copy of the notice and a copy of the full application for probate/administration by registered mail.

   - *(for documents)* I served these documents by sending each person named above a copy of each document listed here together with a copy of the full application for probate/administration by registered mail.

   - I served these documents by personally delivering them to the person named above.

10. Attach the following to Form NC27:

    - If you served notices (NC19, 20, 21, 22, 23, 24, 24.1, or 25), the original notices signed by the executor or administrator.

    - If you served documents (NC1 through NC18), a photocopy of each document.

    - Original post office receipts for sending registered mail.

    - Original courier receipts for documents delivered by courier.

11. Take Form NC27 together with the attached notices and documents to a Commissioner for Oaths. You do not need to go to a notary public unless you live outside of Alberta. Sign Form NC27 in front of the Commissioner.

12. The Commissioner will mark each notice and document as an exhibit to your affidavit according to the list in the NC27. For example, Form NC1 which you have described in your document as "A" will be stamped and marked Exhibit A.

13. The Commissioner will sign, date, and stamp the NC27 as well as each exhibit.

Once everything is completed, make a photocopy of your NC27 and all attachments. When you file this at the court, the clerk will keep the original Form NC27 and stamp the copy for your records.

Sample 35
Form NC27

NC27

COURT FILE NUMBER	123456
ESTATE NAME	Frederick French
DOCUMENT	**Affidavit of service**
DEPONENT'S NAME	Janet French

THE DEPONENT SWEARS UNDER OATH OR AFFIRMS THAT THE INFORMATION IN THIS AFFIDAVIT IS WITHIN THE DEPONENT'S KNOWLEDGE AND IS TRUE. WHERE THE INFORMATION IS BASED ON ADVICE OR INFORMATION AND BELIEF, THIS IS STATED.

On _____October 22, 2011_____, I served true copies of the originals of the following
(date)
documents:

Attached as Exhibit Document
    A NC19 Notice to beneficiary (residuary) — John French
    B NC20 Notice to beneficiary (non-residuary) — Monique French

on the following (insert names and addresses of those served):

John French	Monique French
33 Third Street	44 Fourth Street
Windsor, ON	Winnipeg, MB
N9A 9A9	R3C 3R3

By sending each of the named beneficiaries the notice together with a copy of the full application for probate by registered mail.

Attached as Exhibit C are the registered mail receipts from the post office dated
_____October 22, 2011_____.
(date)

SWORN OR AFFIRMED BY THE DEPONENT	)	
BEFORE A COMMISSIONER FOR OATHS	)	
AT _____CALGARY, ALBERTA_____ ON	)	_____*Janet French*_____
(city/province)	)	Signature of deponent
_____OCTOBER 24, 2011_____.	)	
(date)	)	
	)	
	)	
_____		
Signature of Commissioner		

_____
Appointment Expiry Date

13

Creditors
and Claimants

1. Who Are Creditors and Claimants?

A creditor or claimant is a person or business who believes that the deceased owes them money. Examples might include —

- someone who sold goods to the deceased, but the deceased had not yet paid in full for the purchase;

- someone who provided housekeeping, home-care, or companionship services to the deceased and had not yet been paid; or

- someone who loaned the deceased money for which the deceased gave an IOU or a promissory note.

If the creditor or claimant can prove the debt (that is, prove that the amount claimed was really owing), he or she can make a claim against the estate so that the estate will have to repay the debt. It is more likely that there will be a creditor or claimant if the deceased was actively running a business at the time of his or her death.

2. The Notice to Creditors and Claimants

The Notice to Creditors and Claimants is a one-paragraph notice that appears in the Legal Notice section of newspapers. Its purpose is to let the public know that a person has died so that if someone wants to make a claim, he or she can do so.

It is not required by law that a Notice to Creditors and Claimants be published in every estate. It is up to the executor to decide whether or not it is going to be published. When deciding whether or not to publish the Notice, consider the likelihood that the deceased could have unknown debts. Each estate is different and your decision will rest on the facts and your assessment of the potential risk of a debt being unknown. In cases where the executor had been handling the deceased's affairs under an Enduring Power of Attorney for several years, the executor might feel quite confident that there are no such creditors. An executor who has little knowledge of the deceased's financial affairs might be less sure.

Publishing the Notice to Creditors and Claimants can protect the executor against an unknown creditor who shows up later, after all of the assets of the estate have been given to the beneficiaries and there is nothing left in the estate. The executor could be personally liable to a legitimate creditor who just found out about the death. If the executor can show that he or she took reasonable steps to find all creditors by publishing the Notice, then the executor is in a much stronger position and will likely not end up being personally responsible for the debt.

If the sole beneficiary of the estate is also the executor, it is probably unnecessary to advertise.

You will have to decide for yourself whether you want to publish the Notice. If you are applying to be an administrator rather than the executor, you cannot legally advertise for creditors and claimants until you have the Grant of Administration from the court.

There is a charge for placing a notice in the paper, and many executors are unpleasantly surprised by how expensive this can be. An executor or an administrator who has already received a Grant of Administration may use estate funds to pay for this, if there are such estate funds.

3. When and Where to Put the Notice in the Newspaper

If you are going to publish a Notice to Creditors and Claimants, you must choose a newspaper in Alberta that is circulated in the area where the deceased usually lived. It can be either a daily newspaper or a weekly. You must also complete Form NC34, which is the form required under the Rules of Court.

If the gross value of the estate is $100,000 or less, you only have to publish the Notice once. If the gross value of the estate is more than $100,000, publish the Notice twice in the same paper. Leave one week or more between the two publication dates. The usual procedure is to publish on the same day for two consecutive weeks. For example, your notice might appear in the Tuesday paper one week as well as the Tuesday paper of the following week.

To know whether the estate is over or under $100,000, look at the NC7 Inventory of property and debt that was prepared as part of the Application for Probate or Application for Letters of Administration, as described in Chapter 7. Make sure you look at the gross value and not the net value.

4. How to Prepare the Notice to Creditors and Claimants (Form NC34)

Follow these steps to complete your Form NC34:

1. Fill in the name of the deceased, making sure that you match the name as it appeared in the Form NC1 application.

2. Fill in the date that the deceased passed away.

3. Fill in the date that is the last day a creditor or claimant can come forward with a claim. You have to calculate the date yourself. Once you have decided which days your notice will appear in the newspaper, add at least 30 days after the second notice will appear. For example, if your notice is going to be published on Tuesday, November 4th and Tuesday, November 18, the date for the deadline has to be at least 30 days after November 18.

4. Fill in your name and mailing address.

Once this form has been completed, telephone the newspaper you have chosen and ask the staff of the legal notices department (part of classified advertisements) for a fax number that you can use to send in your Form NC34. Make sure that you state specifically which days you want your notice to appear. Be reasonable with your request; you cannot get a notice in to the paper on the same day you fax your notice to them, and likely not the next day either. Be sure to give them a few days to process your request.

See Sample 36 for an example. There is also a blank Form NC34 on the CD.

5. Statutory Declaration of Publication

Once you have placed your advertisements, you have to obtain proof that the advertisements were properly placed. That proof comes in the form of a Statutory Declaration of Publication. This refers to a one-page document that is sworn by an employee of the newspaper attesting

Sample 36
Form NC34

NOTICE TO CREDITORS AND CLAIMANTS

Estate of ___Samuel Winston France___ who died on _____October 1, 2011_____

If you have a claim against this estate, you must file your claim by ___February 1, 2012___
and provide details of your claim with

_____Lillian France_____
(name of executor)
___4550 – 450 Avenue___
___Edmonton, Alberta___
___T5T 5T5___
(address of executor)

If you do not file by the date above, the estate property can lawfully be distributed
without regard to any claim you may have.

to the dates your notice was published. A copy of your published notice is attached as an exhibit to the Statutory Declaration.

Larger newspapers, such as those in major cities, are very familiar with this procedure and may supply you with the Statutory Declaration of Publication automatically a few days after your notice has finished running.

If you are advertising in a smaller local paper, the staff may not have dealt with as many Notices to Creditors and Claimants and may not be as familiar with the Statutory Declaration. In that case, you may have to ask them for one and supply the form of document. The form used is Form NC34.1.

A Form NC34.1 Statutory Declaration of Publication is included in Sample 37 and on the CD. Follow these steps to complete your Form NC34.1 (note that you, the executor or administrator, are called "the declarant" in Form NC34.1 as you are the person who is declaring something to be true):

1. Fill in the court file number from the backer of your application.

2. Fill in the judicial district from your Form NC1 application.

3. Fill in the estate name exactly as it shows on Form NC1.

4. Fill in your name and address in paragraph 1.

5. In paragraph 2, fill in the name of the newspaper that carried your two published notices.

6. Also in paragraph 2, fill in the name of the city, town, or county where the notices appeared.

7. In paragraph 2.1, fill in the date that the notice was published the first time.

8. In paragraph 2.2, fill in the date that the notice was published the second time.

9. If you are only publishing your notice once because the estate is valued at less than $100,000, leave out paragraph 2.2.

10. Cut your published Form NC34 out of the newspaper and staple or tape it to a regular 8.5″x 11″ piece of paper (or print one off from your computer).

11. On the front of the piece of paper that has your notice, type or neatly print the words "This is Exhibit "A" to the Declaration of _____, declared before me at the City/town of _____ in the Province of Alberta, on _____." Fill in your name in the first blank. Then fill in the town or city you live in and the date that you take your document to a Commissioner for Oaths.

12. Staple the Exhibit A page to the Form NC34.1 page.

13. Take both pages to a Commissioner for Oaths and declare it to be true. The Commissioner will sign and stamp both pages.

14. Make a copy of the signed and stamped document.

15. Take your document to the Clerk of the Court for filing. He or she will keep the original and stamp the photocopy. You will keep the photocopy for your records.

6. What to Do If You Are Notified of a Claim

After publication of your Notice in the newspaper, you may be contacted by a creditor or claimant who says that the deceased owed him or her money. If you believe the claim is valid, you can accept it and pay it when funds become available. If you are not prepared to accept any particular claim without proof, the creditor or claimant has to prove his or her claim by producing receipts, work orders, written agreements, or whatever paperwork is applicable.

If you are satisfied that it is a valid claim and you have not yet filed your application, you will list the claim on the list of debts on the NC7 Inventory. Whether or not the claim is listed there, you will pay out the creditor or claimant as you would pay any other bill or expense, when estate funds become available. Be fair with the creditor or claimant by

Sample 37
Form NC34.1

NC34.1

COURT FILE NUMBER

COURT   **Court of Queen's Bench of Alberta**
                                    (Surrogate Matter)

JUDICIAL DISTRICT   Edmonton

ESTATE NAME   William Brown, a.k.a. Bill Brown

DOCUMENT   **Statutory Declaration of Publication**

EXHIBIT ATTACHED   **Advertisement**

THE DECLARANT SOLEMNLY DECLARES THAT THE INFORMATION IN THIS STATUTORY DECLARATION IS WITHIN THE DECLARANT'S KNOWLEDGE AND IS TRUE. WHERE THE INFORMATION IS BASED ON ADVICE OR INFORMATION AND BELIEF, THIS IS STATED.

1. The declarant's name and complete address is _____ Sarah Brown, 121 First Avenue, Edmonton, Alberta, T1T 1T3 _____.

2. The declarant states that, on examination of the _____ Edmonton Journal _____, a
   (name of newspaper)
   newspaper published in _____ Edmonton _____, Alberta, true copies of the attached advertisement, marked as Exhibit A, appeared in the following issues of the newspaper:

   2.1 _____ October 1, 2011 _____
           (first date of publication)

   2.2 _____ October 14, 2011 _____
           (second date of publication)

DECLARED BEFORE A COMMISSIONER FOR OATHS AT _____ EDMONTON _____,
ALBERTA, ON _____ NOVEMBER 1, 2011 _____.

_____*Sarah Brown*_____   _____
      Declarant   Commissioner's Name

                                       _____
                                       Appointment Expiry Date

advising him or her if there is to be a delay in payment. For example, if the deceased's home must be sold first to make funds available, let the creditor know that it may take a few months before you have estate funds.

If you do not believe that it is a valid claim, or believe that the amount claimed is wrong, you can contest the claim by filing and serving a Form C11, Notice of contestation. If you do serve a creditor or claimant with this notice, he or she has sixty days to come up with proof of the right value. If he or she does not do that within the time allowed, the claim is forever barred and the estate does not have to pay it.

Follow these steps to complete your Form C11:

1. Fill in the Court File Number, Judicial District, and Estate Name as they appear on your Form NC1.

2. Below the solid line, fill in the name and full address of the claimant whose claim you dispute.

3. In paragraph 1, fill in the name of the estate.

4. In paragraph 1.1, describe the claim in a few words (e.g., "unpaid services").

5. In paragraph 1.2, fill in the dollar amount that the claimant is asking for (even if you do not agree it is a reasonable amount).

6. Sign and date the document on the lines provided.

7. Fill in your name, address, telephone number, and fax number below your signature.

8. Make two photocopies of the signed form.

9. Take the original and one copy of the form to the Clerk of the Court to be filed. The Clerk will keep the original and give you back the copy with a court stamp on it.

10. Send the court-stamped copy of the form along with the sections of the *Administration of Estates Act* and the Surrogate Rules (both included in this kit) to the claimant by registered mail.

A copy of Form C11 can be found on the CD-ROM.

14

Recording Financial Transactions

As an executor, you must keep detailed records of your work and efforts on behalf of the estate, as well as your expenses. At the end of your work on the estate, you will be required to present a full accounting of every transaction you made with estate money, and the better your ongoing records, the easier that accounting will be. Keep in mind that as an executor, you may be required to repay any losses that result from your carelessness or errors, so it is best to keep all receipts, work orders, invoices, emails, cancelled cheques, and any other financial paperwork that will help you explain the various transactions in the estate.

This chapter will give you information on what records you need to keep and some ideas about how best to keep them organized. Your recording does not have to be elaborate or complicated; it just has to be consistent and accurate.

1. What Records Must I Keep?

You will be able to produce and keep most of your financial records on your computer if you want to. However, there is a lot of paperwork generated by outside sources on an estate, so you will have to be prepared to deal with that.

Set up a series of paper folders and label them as needed according to the details of the estate you are working on. You will need, at the very least, folders for the following:

- Taxation
- Inventory
- Executor's bank account
- Personal and household items
- Estate assets
- Estate debts
- Financial records
- Estate documents

In the taxation folder, you should keep:

- Tax returns for previous years for the deceased
- Copies of any tax returns filed while you are executor
- Copies of T4, T5, or other tax slips received
- Receipts for any charitable donations made under the will
- Any tax materials that you are collecting, for when it is time to have the tax return prepared
- Letters to and from accountants regarding taxes
- Bills paid to accountants or tax preparers
- Copies of cheques to an accountant or to Canada Revenue Agency
- Notice of Assessment from Canada Revenue Agency
- Tax Clearance Certificate

In the inventory folder, you should keep:

- A copy of the Form NC7 Inventory of property and debt you filed with your application
- Copies of all letters you wrote to banks, insurance companies, credit card companies, etc., to determine values of assets and debts
- The replies received to your letters
- The bill for appraisers or evaluators you hired to help with the inventory

- Any other paperwork that backs up the descriptions, numbers, or values you used to prepare the NC7 inventory

In the executor's bank account folder, you should keep:

- Paperwork used to open the account

- Paper statements received (if you use online banking only, print a copy about once a month so that you have a record of bank charges, interest payments, automatic debits and credits, etc.)

- Cancelled cheques written on the account

- A copy of each transaction in which interest from an investment is paid into the account

- A copy of each transaction in which an account, investment, pension plan, or other financial instrument was cashed in and paid to the account

In the personal and household items folder, you should keep:

- A list of each item taken by each beneficiary

- Registration papers for vehicles, tractors, etc.

- VIN numbers and serial numbers

- Any lists prepared by auctioneers or estate sales agents

- A copy of any payments made to auctioneers or estate sales agents

- A copy of valuation of any collections, memorabilia, antiques, etc.

- Notes regarding money made at a garage sale or yard sale

- A list of items donated to charities, and any receipts for same

You may find it useful to further break down the estate assets folder, depending on what you have to deal with. It is a good idea to have a separate folder for each piece of real estate in the estate, as each one will be sold or transferred separately. Write the street address or other identifiers on the tab of the folder for quick reference. For each of them, keep in the folder:

- Appraisals

- Copy of title

- Copy of mortgage

- Payout statement for mortgage

- Property insurance papers

- Receipts for payment of property insurance

- Property tax notices

- Receipts for payment of property taxes

- Any written offers received

- All sale documentation, including sale agreement, letter from the lawyer, lawyer's bill, breakdown of the sale transaction, amount paid in commission to the realtor, etc.

You may also want to create separate folders for each bank account or investment portfolio to make record-keeping easier. As each asset is collected, there will be a final statement showing the transfer into your executor's account, so the bank account file will end when the asset has been transferred. In a bank account or investment portfolio folder, you should keep:

- Copies of statements from the deceased's date of death to the day the account is transferred to the executor's account

- Any letters or emails regarding the closing and transfer of the account

If one of the assets of the estate is a business, you will definitely want a separate folder for that. This folder should contain all paperwork pertaining to the business, whether the paperwork deals with tax, assets, debts, or any other matter for which you have made a folder. In this folder, you should keep:

- The minute book for the business (if it is incorporated)

- Any shareholder resolutions made in connection with transfer of the business

- Any shareholder agreement or buy/sell agreement that has a bearing on the transfer of the business

- A list of business assets

- A list of business debts

- The most recent financial statements for the business

- Any correspondence with lawyers, accountants, or business brokers about the transfer of the business

- Any paperwork in connection with a share rollover, farm rollover, estate freeze, or other method of transfer

- Life insurance policies owned by the business on the life of the deceased

- Receipts for money received

- A copy of any transaction where sale proceeds are transferred to the executor's bank account

If the assets of the estate are not large or there are really only one or two assets to deal with, you may choose to use just one assets folder. Do what suits your situation, as long as you stay organized and can find paperwork easily.

In the estate debts file, you should keep:

- A copy of the Notice to Creditors and Claimants

- A copy of any claims received

- Copies of letters from credit card companies, banks, etc., regarding outstanding balances

- Letters from collection agencies

- Copies of any cheques written to pay debts

- Receipts for any payments made

- Letters advising debts have been paid in full

In the financial records file, you should keep:

- A copy of the financial records you prepare for the beneficiaries

- Copies of the release documents prepared for beneficiaries

- The original signed releases returned to you by beneficiaries

- Copies of the letters you sent to the beneficiaries to circulate your financial records to them

- Any correspondence you receive regarding your records, such as requests for more information or more detail

- Executor's time records (see section **3.** for more on this)

- Receipts for executor's expenses

In the estate documents file, you should keep:

- A copy of the Application for Probate or Administration

- A copy of the grant issued by the court

- Notarial copies of the will and the grant
- Certificate of Death and/or Funeral Director's Statement of Death
- A copy of the program from the memorial service
- A copy of the obituary published in the newspaper
- Sympathy cards and letters received

2. Ledger

The backbone of your financial recording is the ledger. If you keep this document up to date and accurate, you should have very few problems with your executor's accounting. The ledger is a document that shows every transaction individually, listed in chronological order and giving a description and a dollar amount. It will form the basis of the Statement of Receipts and Disbursements that you will prepare at the end of the estate when you report to the beneficiaries. To limit the amount of time you have to spend on converting your ledger to a Statement of Receipts and Disbursements, this kit will use just one form for both purposes. You will be able to use your ledger to report to the beneficiaries, rather than preparing a second document.

Many executors assume that bank statements will take the place of a ledger, because the statements are broken down by date and amount. Unfortunately, bank statements rarely contain enough information about the source of deposits or the reason for payments out of an account. As an executor, you must record that extra information.

Ideally, you would set up an executor's bank account as soon as possible, and the ledger will show the transactions into and out of that account. All other bank accounts and investments will be cashed and paid into the executor's account. The proceeds from all assets that are sold will be deposited there, and all bill payments will be paid from there. Make sure you add even small transactions such as interest earned.

The best way to set up your ledger is to make a table that has five columns and can be expanded to include as many rows as you need. The first column is for the dates of the transactions, as you will record each deposit or payment in chronological order. The next column is for recording the dollar amount of all money that comes into the estate, such as the proceeds of the sale of the house or interest earned on invested money. The third column is for recording the dollar amount of every payment made out of the estate, such as for taxes, paying bills, or paying the beneficiaries.

The fourth column is for recording the details of the transaction, and this is where many executors do not do a very good job. This column should contain enough detail so that someone other than you can read it and understand the transaction. The person reading it could be a beneficiary wondering where the money was spent, or an accountant calculating the year's tax return.

Your accounting should include specific details such as:

- The account number for any bank accounts or investments that were cashed in

- The policy number for insurance proceeds received

- The year for which income tax payments or property tax payments were made

- Any work order number for expenses such as renovations to the deceased's home or transport of items to beneficiaries

- Invoice number for payments made

- Account numbers for payments made

- The name of accountants, lawyers, or realtors paid

- VIN number of vehicles sold

The fifth column is a running balance of the estate. A sample Ledger/ Statement of Receipts and Disbursements is included on the CD.

Table 3 illustrates how you might record some of the transactions of an executor's account:

Table 3
Record of Transactions

Date	Received	Paid	Details	Balance
2011-05-15	$2,500		CPP death benefit	$2,500
2011-06-07	$300,000		proceeds of GIC #12345 cashed in	$302,500
2011-06-07	$5,833.27		interest earned on GIC #12345	$308,333.27
2011-06-30		$1,351	paid 2010-11 property tax for the house	$306,982.27
2011-07-05		$11,985.31	paid income tax for 2010	$294,996.96

If the estate goes on for a long time, or if there are several bank accounts and GICs to cash in, you may find your ledger becoming very lengthy. This is normal.

You should update your ledger at least once a month.

3. Executor Expenses and Time

You do not have to claim payment for acting as executor or administrator, but if you think you might want to, you must keep accurate records. Your pay may be based on these records, particularly if there is a dispute by one of the beneficiaries.

Your records here will fall into two categories: time and out-of-pocket expenses. There is no standard hourly rate applicable to executors, but the number of hours spent will add up very quickly, and in the event of a dispute, you need to be able to show the beneficiaries the amount of time it really took you to take care of the estate.

On the CD, you will find a form for keeping track of your time and expenses. When it is time to present your accounting to the beneficiaries at the end of the estate, you may use this document to summarize your efforts and expenses. If any of the beneficiaries request more details, you will be able to very quickly produce them. As with your ledger, you can simply add more rows if you need them.

Table 4 shows an example of how you should record your work, time, expenses, and mileage. An average estate takes up to a year to finalize. In that time, your records will become lengthy, and you will be amazed at how many hours you actually devote to being an executor.

Table 4
Work, Time, Expenses, and Mileage Record

Date	# of Hours Spent	Out-of-Pocket Expenses	Kilometres Driven	Details
2011-08-15	1.5	$17.50	30	met with accountant to discuss tax return; paid for parking downtown for the meeting
2011-08-19	.5			telephone call from beneficiaries
2011-08-22	1.5		210	went to house to check on it
Totals				

4. Personal Property Given to Each Beneficiary

As discussed previously, one of your jobs as executor or administrator is to ensure that the beneficiaries of the estate are given the deceased's personal and household goods that were bequeathed to them. Even though the dollar amount of these items is often significantly smaller than that of the rest of the estate, a huge proportion of estate disputes are about these sentimental items.

The records you keep for these items do not generally form part of the accounting that beneficiaries receive at the end of the estate. However, because it is so well known that disputes over these items are rampant, you should protect yourself by recording all items that are taken with your permission. If valuable or sentimental objects go missing, you will be expected to account for them. You can use your records either to answer the question about who has the missing objects or to establish that the objects were never disposed of with your permission.

5. Who Is Entitled to See the Accounting?

Executors of estates are often inundated with people asking to see the will, the inventory, and various financial documents. This can put the executor in a tough position, because he or she must safeguard the assets of the estate as well as any confidential information. The executor cannot and should not divulge financial information to everyone who asks.

However, the executor can and must account to the residuary beneficiaries of an estate. One of the top reasons executors get into lawsuits or just plain fights with beneficiaries is that they withhold information that the beneficiaries are entitled to receive.

Anybody who is entitled to receive a share of the residue of the estate is entitled to a full accounting from the executor. If your accounting is incomplete or inaccurate, the beneficiaries can use the courts to force you to provide a better accounting or even to remove you as executor. If you are not co-operative with beneficiaries in providing information and you unreasonably put the estate to the cost of legal fees, you will likely find those fees coming out of your executor pay. When the estate ends up in a court fight, the judge decides who is going to pay the legal fees.

6. Can the Beneficiaries Ask to See an Accounting at Any Time?

At any time during the administration of the estate, the residuary beneficiaries can ask you for a full accounting. You should be prepared to provide an accounting at any time, though it is reasonable for you to request a week or so to add last minute transactions. A good way of heading off these requests — which can quickly become onerous and unpleasant — is to voluntarily provide an accounting on a regular basis, perhaps every three months.

15

Transmitting Assets into the Name of the Estate

All assets of an estate must eventually be given to a beneficiary or sold. For some assets, such as real estate and mineral titles, this is done in two distinct steps: transmission followed by transfer. The most common types of assets that must be transmitted using these two steps are discussed in this chapter. Most assets do not need to be transmitted first. If you are dealing with an asset that you do not see described in this chapter, you may skip this step for that asset. Transfer of assets is dealt with in Chapter 20.

The first step is moving the asset from the name of the deceased into your name as executor or administrator. This is known as transmission of the asset and is only a temporary arrangement that allows you to have legal control until you sell or transfer it to a beneficiary. At this point, the executor or administrator does not own the asset but is holding it as a trustee for the beneficiaries of the estate. It is similar to moving the deceased's money into an executor's bank account until the executor uses the money to pay bills or beneficiaries.

The second step is moving the asset from the executor's name into the name of the beneficiary or the buyer. This is referred to as transfer of the asset. The fact that you have to take two steps instead of one does not extend the "executor's year." You are still expected to completely wrap up the estate within a year of the deceased's passing.

Not all estate assets need to go through the transmission step. For example, a vehicle may be sold by the executor as if the executor were the owner, as long as it's not an asset that was bequeathed in a will and as long as the sale proceeds are put into the estate account. There is no intermediary transmission step. If the assets in the estate you are dealing with are not mentioned in this chapter, you do not have to deal with transmission.

1. Real Property

Whether the will directs you to give real estate to a beneficiary or to sell it and share out the proceeds, you must transmit the real estate as your first step. When the deceased was alive, the title to the property was in his or her name. You must transmit the title so that it is in your name as executor. For example, if Sandy Mahon passed away, and her executor, Randy Worth, was going to sell her house, the title to her house would be changed to "Randy Worth, Executor of the Estate of Sandy Mahon."

This gives the executor the legal right to sign documents that change the ownership of the property. It is important for the executor or administrator to understand that this title change is only temporary. It does not allow the executor or administrator to keep the property for himself or herself.

Transmission is not needed for property that is held by the deceased jointly with someone else. It is only needed when the property in question is held by the deceased alone, or where the deceased owned part of a property as a tenant in common. If you are not sure about the title to a particular piece of land, telephone the Land Titles Office at one of the phone numbers at the end of this section and ask for help.

Included in this kit is an example of an Alberta Land Titles Form A, Application For Transmission To Personal Representative. This is the document that you must fill in to transfer any piece of real estate (including mines and minerals titles) to the executor or administrator of the estate. If you are dealing with more than one piece of property, you must fill in a separate Application For Transmission for each one. This form is shown in Sample 38 and is available from the Land Titles Office.

You must have received your Grant of Probate, Grant of Administration, or Grant of Administration with Will Annexed before you file your Application for Transmission, because you will have to attach a copy of your grant to your application. You cannot use a notarized copy for this. You must use a copy that has been certified by the Clerk of the Court of Queen's Bench of Alberta. Although you may send in the original grant if you wish, and the Land Titles Office is willing to return

Sample 38
Land Titles Form A

Alberta
Land Titles

TRA-1
FORM A

**Application For Transmission
To Personal Representative**

Insert name of deceased person from Land Titles records	1)
Select the appropriate box(es)	2) now deceased, is
	a) ☐ the registered owner of
If a) is chosen, insert legal description of the land and, if available, the LINC number	
	(LINC number: _____)
If b) is chosen, list registration number(s) of instrument(s) or caveat(s)	b) ☐ the owner of an interest described in the following instrument of caveat:
	3) I have attached a copy of Probate, Letters of Administration, or Court Order certified by the Clerk of the appropriate Alberta Court.
Insert name and full mailing address, including postal code, of executor or administrator. **If this person is an individual, underline their surname.**	4) The name and address of the Executor or Administrator is
If space is insufficient in any of the areas on this form, insert "See Schedule" in the area and attach a Schedule	5) **I am requesting the Registrar to amend the records at the Land Titles Office to show the Executor of the Will or Administrator of the Estate as the owner of the deceased's estates or interests.**

_____   _____   _____
Date   *Signature*   *Print name of person signing*

√ check one <u>only</u>   ☐ executor OR

☐ administrator OR

☐ lawyer for executor or administrator

?? Have you attached a certified copy of Probate, Letters of Administration or Court Order ??

This information is being collected for the purposes of land titles records in accordance with the Land Titles Act. Questions about the collection of this information can be directed to the Freedom Of Information and Protection Of Privacy Co-ordinator for Alberta Registries, Research and Programme Support, Box 3140, Edmonton, Alberta T5J 2G7, (780) 427-2742.

REG 3075 (98/05)

it, it is not a good idea to release your original document to anyone. If the original is lost, you will have to go back to the court to get a new one.

The Application for Transmission applies to land in Alberta only. If you are trying to transmit land in another province, you will have to contact the land titles or land registry office in that province and obtain the correct forms and instructions.

Follow these steps to fill in the Application for Transmission document:

1. In paragraph 1, fill in the name of the deceased as it shows on the existing title to the land. This is often more complicated than you might think. The name you write in here must be exactly the same in every respect as the name on the title. Even if the name is spelled incorrectly on the title, you must put it in exactly as it is shown. If the name on the Grant of Probate or Administration is different, you must state that they are the same person. For example you might say "Sandy Mahon, in the Grant of Probate called Sandie Mahon."

2. If there is a problem with the name being different, the Land Titles Office may ask you to sign a Declaration Re: Proof of Identity.

3. In paragraph 2, you must describe what the deceased owned. Box "a" refers to title to land, which in almost all cases will be your choice. Box "b" refers to an interest under a caveat. Check off the box that applies.

4. If you check box "a," you must then write or type in the legal description of the land. This can be found on a copy of the title or on the annual municipal property tax certificate. For urban land, the legal description contains a plan, block, and lot number, such as "Plan 1234PK, Block 12, Lot 25." For condominiums, it contains a plan and unit number, such as "Plan 123456, Unit 51." For rural land, it contains a section, township, range, and meridian, such as "SE 24-39-18 W4th" (Southeast quarter of section 24, township 39, range 18, west of the 4th meridian). Any of these kinds of land could have exceptions to the title, so make sure you copy down the whole legal description in its entirety, even if it contains more than is set out in this paragraph.

5. Do not write in the street address or mailing address. It must be the legal description.

6. Also under paragraph 2 is a space for you to include the "LINC number." This number is found on the existing title to the property, usually at the top left-hand corner of the first page.

7. Do not change paragraph 3.

8. Under paragraph 4, write or type in your own name and full address including postal code. Use the name that matches the Grant of Probate or Grant of Administration. For example, if the probate has been issued to Randy Worth, do not fill in this form as R. Worth.

9. Do not change paragraph 5.

10. Near the bottom of the document, you will see a signature line. To the left of that, fill in the date. To the right of your signature, print in your name where indicated.

11. You do not need a witness, nor do you have to swear this document in front of a Commissioner for Oaths.

12. Below your signature, check the box to indicate whether you are an executor or an administrator.

Once the document has been filled in and signed, it must be filed at the Land Titles Office. Alberta is divided into North and South for the purposes of Land Titles and there are offices in Calgary and Edmonton. You can go there in person or mail in your documents and payment. The addresses and telephone numbers are:

Service Alberta Building
710 – 4th Avenue SW
Calgary AB T2P 0K3
(403) 297-6511

John E. Brownlee Building
10365 – 97th Street
Edmonton AB T5J 3W7
(780) 427-2742

The fee charged by the Land Titles Office for filing the Application for Transmission and changing the title to the property is $15 per property. They will give you a copy of each new title, but if you want extra certified copies, they will cost $2 each.

Once the real estate has been transmitted into the name of the executor or administrator, it can be sold to a third party or transferred to a beneficiary of the estate.

2. Mines and Minerals Titles

Rural land all over Alberta has oil and gas exploration and production going on, and often testators will pass minerals titles down through the family. The procedure for transmitting a mines and minerals title is exactly the same as the procedure set out in section **1.** for land titles, except of course the title description will look a bit different. Use the same Application for Transmission form as shown in Sample 38.

Mines and minerals titles tend to be divided and re-divided as they are passed down through generations. The Land Titles Office will not allow a title to be divided into shares smaller than 1/20, so once the title has 20 names on it, no more may be added.

3. Share Certificates (Publicly Traded Companies)

If the deceased owned shares in a portfolio that was administered by a money manager, such as an RRSP that holds stocks and shares, transmission of each individual stock is not required. Section **3.** of this chapter is intended to help you transmit individual share certificates that the deceased may have held at home or in a safety deposit box.

3.1 Transfer agents

The general procedure is that the executor fills in paperwork, has his or her signature guaranteed (see section **3.4** below for more about signature guarantees), then sends the paperwork to a transfer agent. The transfer agent changes the name on the certificates, registers the share ownership with the corporation, and sends the new certificates back to the executor. Unfortunately, not all transfer agents use the same forms, though there are definite similarities in all of them. It is a good idea to contact the transfer agent and request their package of documents. That way, you will get their most up-to-date forms and price list. A sample letter to a transfer agent is included on the CD-ROM. Make sure that you are clear in your letter about whether you are an executor or an administrator, because the documents differ slightly.

To find out which transfer agent you should be dealing with, read the share certificate itself. Usually in very small print near the bottom of the certificate you will see a notation. With older certificates you may find that the notation regarding the transfer agent is out of date and you will have to do some detective work to determine who has taken over for the old, defunct transfer agent.

Though stock transfers must go through a transfer agent, you may be able to get some help from other places. If you are dealing with shares of a bank, you may bring those shares to the bank manager and ask him or her to send the shares directly to the bank's transfer agent. Note that this does not work for other kinds of companies. If you know a stockbroker or financial advisor, you may also ask that person to send the shares to the transfer agent for you.

At the time of preparing this book, the following companies are recognized transfer agents in Canada:

Alliance Trust Company
#450, 407 – 2nd Street SW
Calgary, AB T2P 2Y3
Phone: (403) 237-6111
Fax: (403) 237-6181
inquiries@alliancetrust.ca

Capital Transfer Agency Inc.
105 Adelaide St. West, Suite 1101
Toronto, ON M5H 1P9
Phone: (416) 350-5007
Fax: (416) 350-5008
info@capitaltransferagency.com

CIBC Mellon Trust Company (by mail)
PO Box 7010
Adelaide Street Postal Station
Toronto, ON M5C 2W9
Phone: (416) 643-5500 or 1-800-387-0825
Fax: (416) 643-5501

CIBC Mellon Trust Company (by courier)
199 Bay Street
Commerce Court West
Securities Level
Toronto, ON M5L 1G9
Attn: Courier Window

Computershare Trust Company of Canada
100 University Avenue
9th Floor, North Tower
Toronto, ON M5J 2Y1
Phone: 1-800-564-6253 or 514-982-7555

Equity Financial Trust Company
Toronto: Phone: (416) 342-0593
              ddraganjac@equityfinancialtrust.com
              Or phone: (416) 342-0594
              sgilroy@equityfinancialtrust.com
Calgary: Phone: (403) 265-0439
              jcooksley@equityfinancialtrust.com

Vancouver: Phone: (604) 696-4238
              jashbee@equityfinancialtrust.com

Olympia Trust Company
Calgary: 2300, 125 – 9th Ave SE
              Calgary, AB T2G 0P6
              Phone: (403) 261-0900 or 1-800-727-4493
              Fax: (403) 265-1455
Vancouver: 1003 – 750 West Pender Street
              Vancouver, BC V6C 2T8
              Phone: (604) 484-8637
              Fax: (604) 484-8638
Toronto: 920 – 120 Adelaide Street W
              Toronto, ON M5H 1T1
              Phone: (416) 364-8081
              Fax: (416) 364-1827
cssinquiries@olympiatrust.com

Select Fidelity Transfer Inc.
2 Pelham Town Square, Suite 203
Fonthill, ON L0S 1E0
Phone: (905) 892-8118
Fax: (905) 892-0862
joanne@selectfidelity.com

Trans Canada Transfer Inc
25 Adelaide St E., Suite 1301
Toronto, ON M5C 3A1
Phone: (416) 603-4400
Fax: (416) 603-4402
transcanadatransfer@yahoo.ca

Valiant Trust Company
Calgary: 310, 606 – 4th St SW
              Calgary, AB T2P 1T1
              Phone: (403) 233-2801
              Fax: (403) 233-2857
              Toll free: 866-313-1872
Edmonton: 3000 – 10303 Jasper Ave
              Edmonton, AB T5J 3X6
              Phone: (780) 441-2267
              Fax: (780) 441-2247
              Toll free: 1-888-441-2267

Toronto: 1800, 130 King St West
          Toronto, ON M5X 1A9
          Phone: (416) 360-8122
          Fax: (416) 360-1646
          Toll free: 1-888-707-7710
Vancouver: 600 – 750 Cambie St
          Vancouver, BC V6B 0A2
          Phone: (604) 699-4880
          Fax: (604) 681-3067
          Toll free: 1-877-699-4880

3.2   Valueless shares

One of the challenges with transmission of share certificates is figuring out whether the share is actually worth anything. This is especially true with very old share certificates for a company whose name you do not recognize. The company may no longer exist, may have changed its name, or been taken over by another company.

The paperwork is time consuming and transfer agents charge a fee, so often executors and administrators want to know ahead of time whether individual items are worth pursuing. You can usually find this out by going to a website that gives stock quotations to see what the shares are worth. If you know a broker, you can also take the share certificates to him or her to ask about value.

3.3   Declaration of Transmission document

Sample 39 is a blank Declaration of Transmission form. This one is from CIBC Mellon Trust, and will be used as a guide to all Declarations of Transmission.

As mentioned in the previous section of this chapter, it is a good idea to email or call the specific transfer agent you will be dealing with to obtain their forms, as all are slightly different. If you have several different share certificates, you might have to work with more than one transfer agent, as each corporation chooses its own.

To complete the Declaration of Transmission, follow these steps:

1. On the top right-hand side of the form, fill in the name of the deceased as it appears on Form NC1.

2. In the main body of the document, in the first line choose either "I" or "we" and fill in your full name and address. This refers to the executor or administrator who is filling in the document.

3. In paragraph 1, fill in the date the deceased passed away. Cross out either "testate" or "intestate" depending on the facts of your situation.

4. Next to "domiciled at," fill in the full mailing address of the deceased.

5. In paragraph 2, check off the type of grant you received from the court.

6. Below those boxes, cross off the type of representative (e.g., executor, administrator) that does NOT apply to you.

7. Fill in the date the grant of probate or administration was issued to you.

8. Check the box for "court file number" and fill this in using the number shown on the backer of your Form NC1.

9. In paragraph 3, in the first blank, fill in the name of the deceased as it appears on the share certificate. Note this may be slightly different than the name that appears on Form NC1.

10. In the second blank, fill in the name of the company as it appears on the share certificate.

11. In the third blank, fill in the number of shares as it appears in the corner of the share certificate.

12. In the fourth blank, fill in the share certificate number.

13. In paragraph 4, fill in the deceased's name as it appears on the share certificate. In this paragraph, you are stating that the person named in the grant of probate or administration and the person named on the share certificate are the same person.

14. In paragraph 5, fill in the location of the shares on the date of death. For example you could say "safety deposit box at Bank of Nova Scotia in Fort McMurray, Alberta."

15. Do not change paragraph 6.

16. In the final sentence of the document, choose either "I" or "we."

17. Do not sign the document until you are in front of a notary public. The document suggests that a Commissioner for Oaths would be acceptable, but if the document ever leaves the province during the processing of the application, it will be rejected unless it has been notarized. You may save yourself some time and aggravation by having it notarized in the first place.

Sample 39
CIBC Declaration of Transmission Form

CIBC MELLON

DECLARATION OF TRANSMISSION

SHARES
=========

{
{
{   IN THE MATTER OF THE ESTATE OF
{   ....
{   (Full name of the Deceased)
{
{   herein referred to as the "Deceased"

I/We ....
                     (Full name(s) and address(es) of the Personal Representative(s))

....

                              herein referred to as the "Personal Representative(s)",

DO SOLEMNLY DECLARE:

(1) **THAT** the Deceased died on the ....day of .... 20......., testate/intestate, and at the date of death was

domiciled at ....
                                        (Complete Address)

(2) **THAT:**

Court Appointment:

☐ Certificate of Appointment of Estate Trustee (Ontario)

☐ Certificate of Appointment of Succeeding Estate Trustee (Ontario)

☐ Letters Probate/Letters of Administration/Letters Testamentary

☐ Other (specify): ....

was/were granted to the estate trustee(s), executor(s), or other personal representative(s) on

.... (DD/MM/YY)

☐ Court File Number..

☐ ....
                                        (Or Other)

No Court Appointment:

☐ Last Will & Testament

☐ Other (specify): ....

(3) **THAT** there are registered in the name of..
                                        (Insert the name as it appears on face of certificate(s) or share ownership
statement(s))

on the books of ...., the "Company",
                                        (Full name of the Issuing Company)

.... shares of its capital stock,
                                        (Number and class of shares)

represented by certificate(s) or account numbered ....
                                        (Number(s) on certificate(s) or account number on share ownership
statement(s))

DOT_Shares_EN_20100318.doc   Page 1 of 2

Sample 39 — Continued

CIBC MELLON

DECLARATION OF TRANSMISSION

(4) **THAT** the Deceased and ....
(Name on certificate(s) or share ownership statement(s))

named on the said certificate(s) or share ownership statement(s) were one and the same person.

(5) **THAT** the said certificates(s) or share ownership statement(s) was/were at the date of death of the

Deceased physically situated at...
(Insert actual location of share certificate(s) or share ownership statement(s) at the date of death)

and owned by the Deceased.

(6) **THAT** by virtue of the foregoing the said shares have devolved upon and become vested in the declarant(s) as the Personal Representative(s) of the Deceased, who desire(s) to have the same recorded in the name(s) of the Personal Representative(s) upon the register of the Company[1].

AND I/WE make this solemn declaration conscientiously believing it to be true and knowing that it is of the same force and effect as if made under oath and by virtue of "The Canada Evidence Act".

DECLARED[2] before me at ....

in the.......................of.............................

this ....day of .........................A.D.20....................

....
A Commissioner for Oaths, Notary Public
(Affix Notarial Seal or Stamp)

....

....

....
Estate Representative(s) to execute here

---

[1] If Personal Representatives want to have the securities transferred to someone other than themselves, a securities transfer form either on the back of the security certificate or in a separate Securities Transfer Form, must be completed and executed by the Personal Representative(s), and the signatures must be **Signature Guaranteed** to the satisfaction of the transfer agent.

[2] This declaration must be made before a Judge, Notary Public, Justice of the Peace or Commissioner for Oaths authorized to take affidavits to be used in either the Provincial or Federal Courts. Outside Canada, it must be declared before a Canadian Consul or Vice-Consul if possible, otherwise before a Notary Public, who must attach a certificate from the appropriate court as to the fact of his or her being a Notary Public and authorized by law to administer oaths.

DOT_Shares_EN_20100318.doc   Page 2 of 2

Because this form is a declaration, the Notary Public will ask you to declare that the information in the document is true. The declaration has the same legal effect as a document sworn under oath, meaning that giving false information is perjury.

If the shares are being transferred to a beneficiary without being sold first, it is a very good idea to ask the transfer agent to take this step at the same time. It will save you the trouble of going through them twice, as it may be a time-consuming process. If you want to do this, do the following:

1. Turn over the share certificate to find the power of attorney form on the back.

2. Fill in the form (it is brief).

3. Sign the form in front of a signature guarantor.

4. Have your signature guaranteed (see the next section).

When you receive your package of documents from the transfer agent, it will give you instructions about exactly where to send the package of documents as well as any fees that are payable.

3.4 Signature guarantee

Having your signature guaranteed means going to the financial institution where you normally bank and having them stamp your document with a stamp that says "signature guarantee." It is a way for the transfer agent to ensure that someone sees you sign the document in person. Note that in Alberta you can go to any chartered bank, but not a credit union or Treasury Branch. If your own financial institution is not eligible to guarantee your signature, try going to the bank where the deceased had an account.

This is not something that can be done through the tellers; you will have to see the banking officer or manager. Most banks will not charge a fee for this.

The document being guaranteed is the Power of Attorney, not the Declaration of Transmission. Sign the document in front of the banker, who will also sign and affix the stamp. Ensure that the words "signature guaranteed" are visible and legible or the transfer agent will not accept it.

You may be told that you must get a "Medallion signature guarantee." This is an American program that is not used in Canada. Using the Canadian transfer agents listed in this chapter will help cut down on those requests, but you may still have to deal with a transfer agent who asks for the Medallion guarantee. Go through the steps listed here for signature guarantee and it should be accepted without a problem.

When you send in your documentation, be sure to send a notarized copy of the Grant of Probate or Grant of Administration.

4. Canada Savings Bonds

To transmit and transfer Canada Savings Bonds, you must use an Estate Transfer Form, also known as Form 2351. A copy of this form is available from the Canada Savings Bonds office at 1-800-575-5151, or you can email them at csb@csb.gc.ca. You can also download the form and instructions at www.csb.gc.ca. See Sample 40 to see what it looks like.

If the bonds are registered to the deceased and another person with the words "and survivor" or "or survivor," and there is a surviving joint owner of the bonds, do not use Form 2351. The surviving joint owner is responsible for writing to the Canada Savings Bonds office to have the name changed. Your responsibility as executor or administrator will simply be to give the bonds to the surviving joint owner. However, if there are two or more names on the bond and the words "and survivor" or "or survivor" are not there, then you do need to use this form.

4.1 Filling in Form 2351

If a Grant of Probate or Grant of Administration has been issued, fill in sections A, B, C, and F.

If the deceased died leaving a will but no Grant of Probate or Grant of Administration with Will Annexed has been issued, fill in sections A, B, D, and F.

If the deceased died without a will and no Grant of Administration has been issued, fill in sections A, B, E, and F.

In section A, you will be entering information about the deceased. Almost all of this information is found in your application for probate, but you will also need the deceased's social insurance number.

Make sure you fill in the very last part of section A, in which you clarify your position regarding the estate. Indicate that you are an administrator or executor, though you do not have to choose between these two.

In section B, fill in the details of the bonds themselves. You do not need to fill in the bottom two sections unless the bonds were part of a payroll savings program or an RRSP/RRIF. In those cases, you might not have the actual bonds themselves to return.

Section C requires nothing more than checking the box that indicates that a Grant of Probate or Administration was issued and that you are the executor or administrator.

Sample 40
Form 2351

Canada Savings Bonds
the way to save. guaranteed.

[Print Form]

Estate Transfer Form (2351)
and Guidelines

ETRF-06-10
Protected B (when completed)

SPECIFIC INSTRUCTIONS

This form is used for all provinces except Quebec.
Please print clearly or type the required information into the form fields. Please be sure to complete all required Sections to avoid delays in processing your request. Sign page 3 and mail your request to the destination indicated on page 3.

SECTION A - DETAILS REGARDING THE DECEASED AND THEIR REPRESENTATIVES

Full name of the deceased *(list all variations seen within the legal documents. e.g. Death Certificate, Last Will and Testament, Codicil(s))*

Social Insurance Number   Date of death (yyyy/mm/dd)   Last address for the deceased

Civil Status
- ○ Single
- ○ Married
- ○ Other, please specify (e.g., divorce, widow)

City   Prov   Postal code   Country

I / We

Insert full name of all authorized representatives for the deceased
(e.g. spouse, legal estate representative(s), liquidator(s)/executor(s), court appointed administrator(s)/executor(s))

of

Care of address (for estate purposes)   City   Prov   Postal code   Country

do solemnly declare as follows, I am / we are the   ○ Administrator/ Executor(s)

○ Other, please specify (e.g., spouse)   of the deceased named above.

SECTION B - BOND(S)/PLAN(S) DETAILS

The following is a list of all Government of Canada securities (bonds/plans) which were registered to the deceased at the time of death.

	Name(s) appearing on the bond(s)		Registration Account # or Certificate Bond Serial #(s)		$ par value
Canada Savings Bonds / Canada Premium Bonds		AND		AND	
		AND		AND	
		AND		AND	

- The Registration Account # is 10 digits and can be found on a statement or T5.
- The Bond Serial # is located on the top center of the certificate (e.g., CS101F1234567J).

☐ I have attached the physical unsigned certificates to this request.

Total par value $

AND/OR

Payroll Savings Program	Name(s) appearing on the Plan	AND	Plan # (10 digits) [2]	All funds in the plan will be transferred / redeemed

- The 10 digit Plan # can be found on an annual statement or T5.

AND/OR

Canada RSP / Canada RIF	Name appearing on the Plan	AND	Plan # (up to 11 digits) [ ]	All funds in the plan will be transferred / redeemed

- The **Canada RSP** plan number is located on the semi-annual statements
- The **Canada RIF** plan number is located on the quarterly statements

If space is insufficient, please complete and attach a separate sheet that includes the fields seen above. Please initial all attached sheets.

Page 1 of 3 (form)   Canadä

Sample 40 — Continued

[Print Form]

Estate Transfer Form (2351)
and Guidelines

ETRF-06-10

Protected B (when completed)

SECTION C - LETTERS PROBATE OR LETTERS OF ADMINISTRATION

☐ Select this box only if the following situation applies;

Letters Probate / Letters of Administration were obtained and I am / we are the estate's legal representative(s).
The original or a notarial certified copy of the Letters Probate with a copy of the Will attached or Letters of Administration
(with a copy of the Will attached if applicable) issued by the court has been submitted with this request.

SECTION D - TESTATE (DIED WITH A WILL)

☐ Select this box and complete the section below only if the following situation applies;

The deceased left a Last Will dated [   ] which was neither amended nor revoked and no application for
(yyyy/mm/dd)

Letters Probate for the estate has been made or is intended to be made in any jurisdiction.
A notarial certified copy of the deceased Will and Proof of Death that is acceptable to the Bank of Canada is attached.
The following are all the persons, besides myself / ourselves, who are entitled to a share of the securities according to the
Last Will and have consented to the transfer / redemption of the securities by signing below:

Name of the beneficiary		Name of the beneficiary	
Relationship to deceased	Age (if minor)	Relationship to deceased	Age (if minor)
Signature of the beneficiary	WITNESS must sign here	Signature of the beneficiary	WITNESS must sign here

*All signatures must be witnessed and the signatories must be of full age of maturity, qualified and duly authorized (submit tutorship or curatorship documents if
necessary). If space is insufficient, please complete and attach a separate sheet that includes the fields seen above. Please initial all attached sheets.*

SECTION E - INTESTATE (DIED WITHOUT A WILL)

☐ Select this box and complete the section below only if the following situation applies;

The deceased died intestate (without leaving a Last Will and Testament) and no application for Letters of Administration for
the estate has been made or is intended to be made in any jurisdiction.
Attached is a Proof of Death that is acceptable to the Bank of Canada.
The following are all the persons, who are entitled to a distributed share of the securities under the laws respecting intestacy
of the Province in which the deceased was domiciled at the time of death and have consented to the transfer / redemption of
the securities by signing below:

Name of the heir		Name of the heir	
Relationship to deceased	Age (if minor)	Relationship to deceased	Age (if minor)
Signature of the heir	WITNESS must sign here	Signature of the heir	WITNESS must sign here

*All signatures must be witnessed and the signatories must be of full age of maturity, qualified and duly authorized (submit tutorship or curatorship documents if
necessary). If space is insufficient, please complete and attach a separate sheet that includes the fields seen above. Please initial all attached sheets.*

Page 2 of 3 (form)

Canadä

Sample 40 — Continued

Canada Savings Bonds
the way to save. guaranteed.

Print Form

Estate Transfer Form (2351)
and Guidelines

ETRF-06-10

SECTION F - FINAL DECLARATION

In consideration of the transfer or redemption of the securities as requested, I / we undertake to indemnify and save harmless the Bank of Canada against any claim that should at any time arise as a result of such transfer or redemption.
I / we further undertake to administer and utilize the share of each beneficiary or heir only in accordance with the law.
By virtue of the foregoing it is requested that the securities be ☐ **Transferred** and/or ☐ **Redeemed** in favour of the following:

Enter the exact names that are to appear on the NEW bonds/plans or cheque payment (continue on next line if required)

☐ add "*and Survivor*"

Preferred Language of Communication ○ English ○ French	Social Insurance Number (required by income tax legislation)	Date of birth (yyyy/mm/dd)	Series	$ par value

Care of (if applicable)		Address	

City	Prov	Postal code	Country	Home phone (including area code)	Work phone (including area code)

If more than one beneficiary/heir, please complete and attach a separate sheet that includes the fields seen above. Please initial all attachments.

All debts of the estate have been or will be fully paid; I / we hereby undertake to be responsible for the same to the extent of the amount of the above mentioned securities.
I / we give all right, title and interest in the securities described above absolutely and the Bank of Canada is hereby authorized to make such entries in the books of registration as are required to give effect to such transfer/redemption.
I / we make this solemn declaration conscientiously believing it to be true and knowing that it is of the same force and effect as if made under oath and by virtue of the Canada Evidence Act.

Declared before me at _____ City _____ on _____ Date (yyyy/mm/dd)

FINANCIAL INSTITUTION		NOTARY PUBLIC
Place the Financial Institution Signature Guaranteed Stamp or Medallion Guaranteed Stamp in this area	*Signature of all the authorized representative(s)* **must be guaranteed** *by either:* *A Canadian Financial Institution acceptable to the Bank of Canada or by a member of the Medallion guarantee program.* **OR** *Witnessed by a Notary Public, properly identified with the Notary Stamp and Signature of the Notary present.*	*Place the notarial stamp or seal in this area*

Note: The "endorsement guaranteed stamp" is NOT acceptable.

Signature of a Notary Public properly identified above

_____ Signature of legal estate representative _____ Signature of legal estate representative _____ Signature of legal estate representative

Note: Any alterations should be initialed, by the estate representative(s) before the declaration is signed.

Once fully completed, please mail the form, the legal documents and the **unsigned physical certificate bonds** (if applicable) to Canada Savings Bonds, Transfer and Exchange, PO BOX 2770, STN D, Ottawa, ON, K1P 1J7.

For inquiries, contact us by phone at 1 800 575-5151 or at 1 888 646-2626 for Financial Institution, Monday to Friday from 8 a.m. to 8 p.m. ET. We can also be contacted by TTY (teletypewriter only) at 1 800 354-2222.
Please visit us online at www.csb.gc.ca.

Page 3 of 3 (form)

Canadä

In section D, fill in the date of the will. Only use this section of the form if you have not applied for a Grant of Probate or Grant of Administration with Will Annexed and are not planning to apply for either of those. You will have to name the beneficiaries who are entitled to own the Canada Savings Bonds according to the will and fill in their relationship to the deceased and their age. If the will left the bonds to a specific person, include that person's information. If the bonds form part of the residue of the estate, you will have to get each residuary beneficiary to sign Form 2351 and each signature must be witnessed.

In section E, all beneficiaries who are entitled to share in the residue of the deceased's estate must sign the form. Fill in their name, age, and relationship to the deceased. Each beneficiary's signature must be witnessed.

In section F, give your instructions about whether you want the bonds to be transferred or redeemed. "Transferred" means the bonds will be given to a beneficiary without being cashed. "Redeemed" means the bonds will be sold and the money will be placed in the executor's account to be disbursed with the rest of the estate.

If you have chosen "transferred," you must fill in the information about the new owner of the bonds, including name, social insurance number, and date of birth.

Because this form is a declaration, the Notary Public will ask you to declare that the information in the document is true. The declaration has the same legal effect as a document sworn under oath, meaning that giving false information is perjury. Form 2351 has space for both a bank guarantee and a Notary Public's stamp, but you only need one of those. Make sure you sign the very bottom of the form.

4.2 Supporting materials

You will have to send supporting materials along with Form 2351. The requirements depend on the situation, as follows (note that the word "grant" is replaced by "letters" in the form):

1. Grant of Probate or Grant of Administration has been issued. In this case, send:

   a. Form 2351 (filled in, signed, with the signature either witnessed by a notary public or guaranteed by a bank).

   b. Notarial copy of the Grant (make sure a copy of the will is attached, if there is one).

   c. The bond certificate(s).

2. The deceased died with a will but there was no Grant of Probate or Grant of Administration with Will Annexed issued. In this case, send:

   a. Form 2351 (filled in, signed, with the signature either witnessed by a notary public or guaranteed by a bank).

   b. Notarial copy of the will.

   c. Proof of death — any one of: original Certificate of Death, notarial copy of Certificate of Death, original Coroner's Certificate, notarial copy of Coroner's Certificate, original or notarial copy of Funeral Director's Statement of Death.

   d. The bond certificate(s).

3. The deceased died without a will and no Grant of Administration was issued. In this case, send:

   a. Form 2351 (filled in, signed, with the signature either witnessed by a notary public or guaranteed by a bank).

   b. Proof of death — any one of original Certificate of Death, notarial copy of Certificate of Death, original Coroner's Certificate, notarial copy of Coroner's Certificate, original or notarial copy of Funeral Director's Statement of Death.

   c. The bond certificate(s).

Send your package to:

Canada Savings Bonds
Transfer and Exchange
PO Box 2770, STN D
Ottawa, ON K1P 1J7

16

Property That Passes Outside of the Estate

You will discover at the time you prepare the NC7 Inventory that not everything belonging to the deceased becomes part of his or her estate. The distinction of whether or not an item becomes part of the estate is important because only assets in the estate are dealt with by the will. When the deceased owns something that does not become part of the estate and is not covered by the will, that item is said to "pass outside of the estate."

An item that passes outside of the estate does so because certain kinds of assets are owned in ways that already determine who is to own them on the death of the deceased. The two general types of property that pass outside of the estate are —

- jointly owned assets that have an automatic right of survivorship, (such as the items described in section **1.**), and

- assets that have a beneficiary already designated by the deceased (such as in a case where a beneficiary is designated on the asset itself at the time the deceased purchased it).

Some common types of both joint property and designated beneficiary property are discussed in this chapter.

As executor or administrator, you will find that your role is different for these assets than it is for assets in the estate. With assets that pass outside the estate, other people can take steps that otherwise you would have to take. However, keep in mind that as executor or administrator, you should make sure all assets are dealt with and all of the deceased's plans are carried out, even if all you have to do is let someone else know that he or she must take care of an asset.

1. Joint Property

Joint property is not listed on the NC7 Inventory. If the deceased owned any type of property as a joint owner or joint tenant with another person, that other person automatically becomes the owner of the entire asset because joint property carries an automatic right of survivorship. There is no "half" to be listed in the deceased's estate.

The most common types of joint property are real estate, bank accounts, and other savings instruments such as GICs. Always double check the ownership to make sure you know whether a particular asset belongs to the deceased.

If there is joint property that is going to belong to another person now that the deceased has died, send that person a letter (not a phone call) advising them of the death of the deceased. State that you understand they will take the property as a surviving joint tenant. Enclose a copy of the death certificate. There is a sample letter to a surviving joint tenant on the CD.

It is not your responsibility to complete the transfer of a joint asset to the surviving joint owner. He or she is responsible for doing that. Your letter to him or her makes it clear that you are not going to take any steps. With real estate, you cannot take the steps needed even if you want to; the change of title is brought about by a Declaration of Surviving Joint Owner, available from the Land Titles Office.

You do have to provide them with copies of the documentation that they need to transfer the property, however, such as the death certificate.

If your title search alerts you to the fact that the deceased was the joint owner of property but had never removed the other deceased joint owner from the title, see a wills and estates lawyer for help.

2. Life Insurance

At the time you prepared the NC7 Inventory, you examined each life insurance policy to determine who had been named as beneficiary. In this section, we are dealing with insurance policies that do NOT name the deceased's estate and DO name a specific person who is going to receive the proceeds of the policy.

As with joint property, it is not your responsibility to gather the money from the insurance company and give it to the beneficiary. In fact, once the insurance company has received the proper notice of the deceased's death, it will want to deal only with the named beneficiary and probably will not discuss it with you any more.

You should write to the insurance company, citing the policy number if you know it. If you do not have the policy number, give the deceased's name, date of birth, and social insurance number so that they can identify the correct person in their records. All you are doing is notifying them of the death and giving them enough particulars so that they can take care of paying out the claim. You will also send the insurance company a copy of the death certificate. This kit contains a sample letter to the insurance company on the CD.

Occasionally, the insurance company will have some difficulty determining exactly which of the named beneficiaries is entitled to a share. This is not your responsibility to figure out, even if the beneficiaries want you to deal with it. If there is a named beneficiary on a policy, the payout of insurance is a matter of a private contract with the insurance company and there is nothing else you can add to the process.

Life insurance proceeds are not taxable and the estate is therefore not liable for the payment of any tax when the proceeds are paid out to the beneficiary.

3. RRIFs/RRSPs

The money held in a registered retirement savings plan (RRSP) or registered retirement income fund (RRIF) that names a beneficiary is, again, not money that will be paid to you as executor or administrator to deal with. It is your job to notify the plan holder (i.e., the bank, broker, or financial advisor) so that they may take steps themselves. You should let the bank, broker, or financial advisor know in writing and provide a copy of the death certificate.

In one very important way, your role as executor is different with an RRSP or RRIF than it is with life insurance. If the RRSP or RRIF is being rolled over to a spouse, there will be no income tax payable. However, if it is being paid to anyone else, the tax on the full RRSP or RRIF will become payable immediately. This tax has to be paid out of the deceased's estate. The bank or financial house that pays out the funds to the beneficiary will let you know what the tax bill is and will expect you to make the payment out of estate funds.

4. Pension Plans

Your steps with pension plans will be much like those taken with an insurance company. You do not have to write to public pensions such as Canada Pension Plan (CPP). You only need to correspond with private pensions such as those run by the deceased's former employer. There is a sample letter for this purpose on the CD-ROM.

17

Estate Taxes

As mentioned in an earlier chapter, no beneficiaries may inherit under the estate until all debts are paid. Taxes are considered one of those debts. All taxes must be paid before a beneficiary may be paid. As executor or administrator, it is your responsibility to ensure that all required tax returns are filed and that taxes are paid before you pay the beneficiaries their shares. If you should pay the beneficiaries but not the taxes and there is no estate money left, you may be required to pay the estate taxes out of your own money.

1. Inheritance and Death Taxes

In Alberta, there are no death taxes or inheritance taxes. Contrary to popular opinion, the government does not take a percentage of an estate, even if the person dies without a will. The taxes that you as an executor must deal with are income tax and capital gains tax, both of which are described in more detail in this chapter. There is a probate fee that must be paid to the court when you file papers to apply for a Grant of Probate or Grant of Administration, but there is no direct taxation by the government.

2. Why Do Tax Returns?

An estate is considered to be a separate taxpayer just as an individual is. The estate must pay tax on income, and may use deductions and credits

202

to reduce the amount payable. By accepting the role of executor, you step into the shoes of the deceased and his or her estate and must file returns annually (until the estate is wound up) just as the deceased would have done if alive. An executor who fails to do tax returns or files them so late that penalties and interest are incurred may be held personally responsible for paying the extra amounts.

Most estates are wrapped up within a year, so the executor rarely has to prepare more than one estate (T3) return (see Sample 41).

3. Which Returns Do I Do, and When Should I Do Them?

The following are the tax returns that an executor must ensure are prepared and the deadlines for filing them with Canada Revenue Agency:

- A return for the deceased person for the last year of his or her life. That return is called the T1 Individual Terminal Return. For example, if a person died on July 17, 2011, the executor must prepare a tax return from January 1, 2011, to July 17, 2011. This return must be filed on the later of a) the normal filing deadline of April 30 following the death, or b) six months after death.

- A return for any previous tax years that the deceased failed to prepare himself or herself. These are T1 Individual Tax Returns. As they are already overdue, the normal April 30 deadline does not apply. The executor must file them on the later of a) the April 30 following the death, or b) six months after death.

- On some estates, the executor may want to file a "Rights and Things Return." This only applies where there were amounts of money due to the deceased at death, but which had not been paid to him or her yet. This may apply to farmers whose crops had not yet been harvested at the date of death or to self-employed persons who have not yet billed work in progress. This return is due on the later of a) one year after death, or b) 90 days after the assessment date of the T1 Terminal Return.

- A return on behalf of the estate each year until the estate and all of the trusts created by the estate are wound up completely. Those returns are called T3 Trust Returns. The first trust year begins the day after the deceased died and continues for one year. Using the example from above, the trust year for the person who died on July 17, 2011 begins on July 18, 2011 and runs for one year. Each T3 Return is due within 90 days of the end of the trust year.

Sample 41
T3 Trust Return

Canada Revenue Agency / Agence du revenu du Canada

Do not use this area   **2009**

T3 — TRUST INCOME TAX AND INFORMATION RETURN

Legislative references on this return refer to the *Income Tax Act* and *Income Tax Regulations*. All references to "the guide" on this return refer to Publication T4013, *T3 Trust Guide*.

▲ Step 1 – Identification and other required information

Residence of trust at the end of the tax year
Indicate country (if other than Canada)

If Canada, enter the province or territory

Name of trust

Trust account number
T | | | – | | | | | – | |

Name of trustee, executor, liquidator, or administrator

Do not use this area

Mailing address of trustee, executor, liquidator, or administrator

Telephone number

Postal code

Mailing address, if different than trustee (or name and mailing address of the contact person, if different)

Telephone number

Postal code

Is the trust resident on **designated** Aboriginal settlement lands?   No ☐   Yes ☐   If **yes**, enter the name and settlement number.

If the trust had business income in the year, enter the province(s) or territory(ies) where that income was earned.

If the trust became or ceased to be a resident of Canada **in the year**, enter the date.   Became resident   Year | Month | Day   Ceased to be resident   Year | Month | Day

Type of Trust

Testamentary

☐ Spousal or common-law partner

Date of death   Year | Month | Day

☐ Other

Social insurance number of **deceased**

Inter vivos

☐ Spousal or common-law partner

Date trust was created   Year | Month | Day

☐ Unit

☐ Non-profit organization – Business Number:

☐ Mutual fund

☐ Employee trust

☐ Communal organization

☐ Personal trust

☐ Employee benefit plan

☐ SIFT trust (specified investment flow-through trust)

☐ Joint spousal or common-law partner trust

Insurance segregated fund:

☐ Alter ego trust

☐ Fully or partially registered

☐ Other inter vivos (specify)

☐ Non-registered

Deemed resident
Is this a deemed resident trust?   Yes ☐   If **yes**, please indicate any other country in which it is also considered resident.

Return for tax year

from   Year | Month | Day   to   Year | Month | Day

Is this the first year of filing a T3 return?   No ☐   Yes ☐

If **no**, for what year was the last return filed?   Year

If **yes**, attach a copy of the trust document or will, and a list of assets at death (unless filed with the deceased's final T1 return).   Attached ☐   With T1 ☐

Is this an amended return?   No ☐   Yes ☐

Address on last return is same as above, or the following: Same ☐

Is this the final return of the trust?   No ☐   Yes ☐
Year | Month | Day

If **yes**, enter the trust wind-up date.

Your language of correspondence: English ☐   French ☐

Reporting foreign income and property

If the trust is resident in Canada, you have to report its income from all sources, both inside and outside Canada.

If the trust dealt with a non-resident trust or corporation in the year, contact us at **1-800-959-8281** for more filing requirements.

Did the trust hold foreign property at any time in the tax year with a total cost of more than CAN$100,000?   No ☐   Yes ☐

If **yes**, you may have to complete and attach Form T1135, *Foreign Income Verification Statement*. For filing requirements, see that form.

T3 RET E (09)   (Vous pouvez obtenir ce formulaire en français à www.arc.gc.ca/formulaires ou au 1-800-959-3376.)   Canadä

4. Income Tax

Some assets owned by the deceased are tax-deferred (as opposed to tax-free). Common examples of these are RRSPs and RRIFs. The funds put into these plans are pre-tax dollars; in other words, the plan owner has not paid taxes on that money yet. When money is taken out of an RRSP or RRIF, the person who owns the plan and receives the money pays the income on the portion that was taken out.

This rule has an impact on estates because for tax purposes, the deceased is deemed by law to have cashed in his or her plans one minute before he or she died. In other words, the law treats the RRSP or RRIF as if it had been totally cashed out one minute before the deceased died. Since the money has been cashed out, the tax on it must now be paid.

The tax on the RRSP or RRIF has to be paid from the estate even if the proceeds of the RRSP or RRIF are not paid to the estate. For example, the deceased could own an RRSP that holds $250,000, on which he has named his daughter as the beneficiary. When the RRSP is cashed in at the time of death, there is tax of, say, $100,000 owing. The daughter is entitled to receive the entire $250,000. The $100,000 in tax must come out of the other assets of the estate.

5. Capital Gains Tax

When a person passes away, his or her property of all kinds must be transferred either to a beneficiary or to his or her estate. Some of this property is considered to be capital property for tax purposes. For most estates, this includes real estate (homes, cottages, cabins, lake lots, revenue properties, and mines and minerals titles). If a deceased person owned an incorporated business, the shares of the business are also considered to be capital property. There are a few other kinds of capital property as well.

If capital property is worth more when the person dies than it did when he or she first got it, then it has gained in value. This is called a capital gain. The gain is taxable. This means that the gain must be included in the deceased's final personal tax return.

Capital gains tax is calculated as a general rule in this way —

- take the value on the day the person died;

- subtract the value of the property on the day he or she first got it;

- divide the amount in half; and

- add that half to the deceased's tax return.

For example, if Hilary owned a cottage that was worth $100,000 when she bought it but was worth $300,000 when she died, the calculation would look like this:

$$\begin{array}{r} \$300,000 \\ -\ \underline{100,000} \\ \$200,000 \\ \div\ \underline{\qquad 2} \\ \$100,000 \end{array}$$

The amount of $100,000 is added to Hilary's return as income.

This is a very simplified example, as in real life taxes can be much more complicated, but it will give you an idea of what the estate can expect in terms of taxes to be paid.

One very important exception to the capital gains tax rule on property is that it does not apply to a person's principal residence. Each person is entitled to own one home at a time and to sell or pass on that home without any tax.

6. Can I Use an Accountant?

Unless the executor is an accountant or tax preparer by profession, he or she should consider hiring an accountant to prepare the returns. Using an accountant will greatly reduce the chance of an error being made, compared to the return being prepared by an executor unfamiliar with taxation. The accountant will likely also be able to suggest tax-saving strategies such as making a charitable gift in the form of capital property. Also, in the event that a serious error is made, an executor is better off being able to establish that he or she is not responsible for the error because the return was prepared by a professional.

7. What Is a Tax Clearance Certificate?

A Clearance Certificate is a written notice from Canada Revenue Agency (CRA) which proves that all taxes owing have been paid by an estate. The idea of it is to let an executor know that it is now safe to distribute the rest of the estate to the beneficiaries. CRA does not issue the Clearance Certificate automatically; it is the executor's responsibility to apply for it or to ask the accountant to apply for it when the tax returns are sent in.

If you, as an executor, do not wish to apply for a Clearance Certificate, you cannot be forced to apply for one. It is up to you. However, it is good protection for you in the event that more taxes are levied later and you have already distributed the whole estate. Most executors choose to have the protection.

It can take months to get a Clearance Certificate. You should probably warn the beneficiaries to expect a six-month wait for it. Also let them know that there is nothing you can do to hurry CRA. You will likely find that the beneficiaries of the estate are unwilling to wait for the Clearance Certificate and will demand that you pay them before it is issued. If you believe it to be a good idea, you may choose to make an interim distribution of the estate while you are waiting. Again, this is your choice. You must weigh the risks yourself.

If you want to make an interim distribution, you can do so by holding back enough money to pay the upcoming taxes and any final expenses such as legal fees, your out-of-pocket expenses, and anything else yet unpaid. Prepare the final accounting as set out in Chapter 19 and present the full set of documents to the beneficiaries. Before any beneficiary is paid, make sure every beneficiary has given you a signed release. You can then pay out the interim amount to the beneficiaries. Once you receive the Clearance Certificate you can pay them the rest.

Be sure to assess your risks carefully before you go ahead with an interim distribution. Remember that it is better to overestimate what the taxes will be than to underestimate and leave the estate short of money.

See Sample 42 for an example of the government form used to request a Clearance Certificate (available from www.cra-arc.gc.ca).

Sample 42
Asking for a Clearance Certificate

■+■ Canada Revenue   Agence du revenu
Agency   du Canada

ASKING FOR A CLEARANCE CERTIFICATE

Use this form if you are the legal representative for an estate, business, or property and you are asking for a clearance certificate. A legal representative includes an executor, administrator, liquidator, trustee, or like person other than a trustee in bankruptcy.

Send this form to the Assistant Director, Audit, at your tax services office. Do **not** attach this form to the return. You can find the address of your tax services office on our Web site at **www.cra.gc.ca/contact**.

Do **not** send us this form until:

- you have filed all the required tax returns and have received the related notices of assessment; and
- we have received or secured all income taxes (including the provincial or territorial taxes we administer), Canada Pension Plan contributions, Employment Insurance premiums, and any related interest and penalties.

Attach to this form the documents listed below to help us issue the certificate without delay:

- a copy of the will, including any codicils, renunciations, disclaimers, and all probate documents (If the taxpayer died intestate, also attach a copy of the document appointing an administrator and details of the proposed distribution of assets, including the names, addresses, and social insurance numbers or account numbers of the beneficiaries, and his or her relationship to the deceased.);
- a copy of the trust document;
- a statement showing the properties and the distribution plan, including the date chosen for the distribution of properties, and a list of the recipients of each of the properties (for each property, provide a description, the adjusted cost base, and the fair market value at the date of death or distribution);
- any other documents that are necessary to prove that you are the legal representative; and
- a letter of authorization that you have signed if you want us to communicate with someone else.

For more information, refer to the Information Circular 82-6, *Clearance Certificate* or call **1-800-959-8281**.

DO NOT USE THIS AREA

Identification area
Name of deceased, corporation, or trust, whichever applies

Address

Social insurance number, Business Number, or trust number, whichever applies	Date of death **or** date of wind-up, whichever applies

Legal representative's name (if there is more than one, please provide the details on a separate sheet)

Legal representative's address (we will send the clearance certificate to this address)

Legal representative's capacity (for example, executor, administrator, liquidator, or trustee)	Telephone number

---

Period covered

I am asking for a clearance certificate for the period ending _____
(The period ending date is the date that all the obligations or duties of the will or other final document of the deceased have been satisfied.)

Tax returns filed

Have you filed any tax return(s) for the year of death?   ☐ Yes   ☐ No

If *yes*, indicate what type of tax return(s) you filed. For more information, get guides T4011, *Preparing Returns for Deceased Persons*, T4012, *T2 Corporation Income Tax Guide*, and/or T4013, *T3 Trust Guide*.

☐ T1 final return   ☐ T1 return for rights or things   ☐ T2 Corporation Income Tax Return

☐ T1 return for income from a testamentary trust   ☐ T1 return for partner or proprietor   ☐ T3 Trust Income Tax and Information Return

---

Certification and undertaking

I am asking for a clearance certificate from the Minister of National Revenue. The certificate will certify that all taxes (including provincial or territorial taxes administered by the Canada Revenue Agency), Canada Pension Plan contributions, Employment Insurance premiums, and any related interest and penalties for which the deceased, corporation, or trust named above is liable (or can reasonably be expected to become liable) have been paid or that the Minister has accepted security for the amounts. The certificate will apply to the tax year in which the distribution is made and any previous year for which I am liable (or can reasonably be expected to become liable) as the legal representative of the deceased, corporation, or trust identified. I will complete the distribution of all of the property as soon as possible after I receive the clearance certificate.

Date	Capacity (for example, executor, administrator, liquidator, or trustee)	Signature
Date	Capacity (for example, executor, administrator, liquidator, or trustee)	Signature

TX19 (09)   (Français au verso)   **Canadä**

18

Executor or Administrator Compensation

1. Can I Be Paid for Being an Executor or Administrator?

The general rule is that executors and administrators are entitled to be paid a wage for their time and efforts in looking after someone's estate. The wage is over and above any reasonable out-of-pocket expenses that you might have incurred while acting as executor. See section **6.** in this chapter regarding which expenses you can expect to be reimbursed by the estate.

Executor's and administrator's fees are earned income, and therefore are taxable. You have to include any amount you receive in fees on your personal income tax return for the year the fees are paid to you.

2. How Much Should I Be Paid?

If a will states how much an executor is to be paid, then the executor should expect that as his or her maximum payment (not counting expenses). The executor can only ask for more than the amount stated in the will if the court orders it or if all residuary beneficiaries of the estate agree to it.

Not all wills say something about the amount of payment. In those cases, the executor will have to figure out how much he or she thinks is fair payment, then ask the residuary beneficiaries to agree to it. There is no standard hourly dollar rate.

The accepted range of compensation for an executor or administrator on an average estate is between 1 and 5 percent of the value of the estate. The value is taken from the Form NC7 inventory. The executor will have to figure out where he or she fits in that range. As a general rule, the more complex, large, and time-consuming an estate, the higher the compensation should be. If the executor has had to take care of extra work such as an estate lawsuit, he or she will be able to claim a wage for that additional work that is outside the usual range.

The Alberta Surrogate Rules, which govern probate matters, say that the following factors should be considered when the amount of executor's or administrator's pay is being set (note that the words "personal representative" mean either an executor or an administrator) —

- the gross value of the estate;
- the amount of revenue receipts and disbursements;
- the complexity of the work involved and whether any difficult or unusual questions were raised;
- the amount of skill, labour, responsibility, technological support, and specialized knowledge required;
- the time expended;
- the number and complexity of tasks delegated to others; and
- the number of personal representatives appointed in the will.

Additional compensation may be allowed when personal representatives encounter the following situations —

- are called upon to perform additional roles in order to administer the estate, such as exercising the powers of a manager or director of a company or business,
- encounter unusual difficulties or situations, or
- must instruct a lawyer to deal with litigation.

3. How Does Payment Work If There Is More Than One Executor?

If the will states that each executor is to receive a certain amount, then the instructions in the will should be followed.

If there is nothing in the will about that, the amount calculated as being in the 1 to 5 percent range must be split among all the executors or administrators. This is not necessarily an equal split, as quite often one executor will do more of the work than the other. The executors may agree between themselves on the proportions of the split as long as they do not exceed the appropriate total.

4. When Do I Get Paid?

Payment is made to an executor or administrator at the end of the work on the estate. This could be months or even a year from the time you first start work. If there is a will that states that the executor can "pre-take" payment, then the executor can pay himself or herself part of the wage when a portion of the work is done, even though the estate might not be finished. Usually, executors and beneficiaries get paid at the same time.

5. How Do I Get Paid?

When the estate is ready to wrap up and the executor is about to pay the beneficiaries their final shares, he or she should present the residuary beneficiaries with financial statements of what has happened in the estate. Part of those financial statements will be the executor or administrator's request for payment. Note that this step is taken before the beneficiaries receive their money but after all estate property has been gathered in and all taxes and expenses have been paid.

The executor or administrator then asks the beneficiaries to approve in writing the financial statements. This is done by the beneficiaries signing a release that the executor or administrator has prepared (see Chapter 19 for more about releases). If all of the beneficiaries sign and return their releases, the executor or administrator may write himself or herself a cheque for the amount requested in the financial statements.

If the beneficiaries do not agree to the proposed amount, the executor or administrator may try to negotiate an amount that suits everyone. If that is not possible, the only resort left for the executor or administrator is to ask the court to set the amount of compensation.

6. What Expenses Can I Claim?

Estate expenses are very poorly understood. Contrary to popular belief, the estate is not responsible for paying for the hotels, airfares, and meals of family members attending the deceased's funeral. Each person is responsible for taking care of that themselves. The executor is in a unique position, whether or not the other family members understand that or agree with it.

The general rule is that an executor alone is to be reimbursed for all reasonable expenses he or she incurs on behalf of the estate while looking after the estate. This can be abused, intentionally or otherwise, and leads to many disputes. An executor who is from out of town can expect to be reimbursed for reasonable travel, accommodation, and meal expenses to take care of estate tasks.

Some acceptable expenses include:

- Economy airfare for the executor

- Mileage and parking for the executor to attend appointments related to the estate, such as lawyers, accountants, realtors, appraisers, bankers, or funeral directors

- Reasonable meals for the executor while on the road on estate business

- Photocopies of estate documents

- Faxing of documents or statements to professionals assisting with the estate

Some unacceptable expenses include:

- Airfare, accommodations, and meals for the executor's family to accompany him or her on estate business

- Entertainment for the executor

19

Preparing Final Financial Statements for Distribution

One of your final projects as an executor or administrator is to prepare a set of financial statements that paint a picture of everything you did on the estate. The statements will be presented to the residuary beneficiaries of the estate for approval. You need the approval to receive your executor's pay, to pay the beneficiaries their share, and to know that nobody is going to contest what you have done with the estate.

The financial statements are prepared once all assets have been collected, assets to be sold have been sold, tax returns have been done, and all debts and expenses have been paid. In other words, there is probably nothing left to be done except pay out the money and receive the Clearance Certificate. This is the point where you are ready to give the money to the beneficiaries and all you need is their approval of what you have done with the estate.

It is important to understand that if you as an executor or administrator have been negligent or fraudulent with the estate's money or are unable to account for it, you may be required to pay back estate money out of your personal assets. You are able to relieve this burden by having each beneficiary state in writing (i.e., sign a release) that they are satisfied with the work you have done. You get that release by preparing the financial statements to show how you have settled the estate. If you skip this process, you may get a surprise years from now when a beneficiary decides that he or she is unhappy with what he or she received from the estate.

This chapter will show you how to prepare the financial statements you will send to the beneficiaries before giving them their money. Along with the step-by-step instructions, there is a sample estate that is used throughout the chapter to illustrate the steps. Our sample estate documents are much shorter and less detailed than yours are likely to be.

1. What to Do with the Financial Statements Once They Are Prepared

Here is the basic blueprint for making and using the financial statements that you will prepare in this chapter:

1. Prepare the financial statements described below (i.e., the statement of receipts and disbursements, the statement of proposed executor's compensation, and the statement of proposed distribution).

2. Prepare a release for each residuary beneficiary.

3. Give each residuary beneficiary a copy of the statements and a release. A sample letter is enclosed.

4. Wait for signed releases from all beneficiaries before paying anyone.

5. Once all releases are received, pay yourself and the beneficiaries out of the executor's account.

2. Statement of Receipts and Disbursements

In Chapter 14, you set up a document called "Ledger/Statement of Receipts and Disbursements." In this chapter, you will use that same document as an important part of the final financial reporting.

Your Statement of Receipts and Disbursements will list all the deposits and payments made in the estate. To finish it off, do the following:

1. Total the "received" and the "paid" columns. If you subtract the "paid" from the "received," you should end up with the same total that shows in your "balance" column. In the example below, $423,356.27 - 17,246.00 = $406,110.27. If it does not work out exactly, something is missing. The items that are missed most often are smaller ones such as bank charges and interest earned. Also check that each item is in the right column. Double check your work to make it balance.

2. Check that the balance shown on your document (in this case, $406,110.27) is also the total of the actual bank account. If you have

more than one account or you have an account and investments, add them together to get the same number as is shown on your statement. After all, the point of the Statement of Receipts and Disbursements is to accurately reflect what is in the estate.

3. Add the date on the same row as the totals. All of your documents that go out to the beneficiaries should be dated the same day.

See Table 5 and Sample 43.

Table 5
Ledger of Receipts and Disbursements

Date	Received	Paid	Details	Balance
2011-09-12	$2,500	$0	received CPP death benefit	$2,500
2011-09-14	$45,856.27	$0	cashed in GIC	$48,356.27
2011-09-14	$0	$10,255	paid funeral bill	$38,101.27
2011-09-19	$375,000	$0	sold the house	$413,101.27
2011-09-22	$0	$6,991	paid 2010 income tax owing	$406,110.27
2011-11-03	**$423,356.27**	**$17,246**		**$406,110.27**

3. Statement of Proposed Executor's Compensation

The purpose of this statement is to claim what you think is a fair amount of compensation for your time and efforts as executor or administrator and to explain how you arrived at that amount. You should have two sections: your wage and your out-of-pocket expenses. See Sample 44 for an example.

Once again, you will start with the records that you have been keeping during your time as executor. Specifically, the chart you've been using to track your time and expenses on the job (Table 6). This is another of the forms you began in Chapter 14. Total the columns for number of hours spent on estate work, out-of-pocket expenses, and number of kilometres driven. Be sure to add in anything that you have not yet paid for or done, but that you know you will have to do. For example, add in the time it is taking to prepare and distribute your financial records and the time it will take to prepare and send out the cheques once you have received the releases.

Sample 43
Statement of Receipts and Disbursements

Statement of Receipts and Disbursements

Estate of Mary Marie Walker

Date	Received	Paid	Details	Balance
2011-08-18	$2,500		received CPP death benefit	$2,500
2011-08-22	$18,774.25		transferred Mom's bank account at CIBC into executor's account at TD	$21,274.25
2011-08-23		$8,736.29	paid funeral bill	$12,537.96
2011-09-16		$8,516	paid legal fees including probate fee	$4,021.96
2011-10-10	$347,511		sold the house	$351,532.96
2011-10-29	$4,900		sold the car	$356,432.96
2012-01-19		$1,253.14	paid 2010 income tax owing	$355,179.82
2012-02-06	$212,995.44		cashed in investments	$568,175.26
2012-02-06		$84.99	paid final phone bill	$568,090.27
2012-02-06		$750	paid caregiver's last wages	$567,340.27
Totals	**$586,680.69**	**$19,340.42**		

Hint: Check your math. Money received ($586,680.69) minus money paid out ($19,340.42) must equal the balance left in the account = $567,340.27.

Sample 44
Statement of Proposed Executor's Compensation

In the Estate of _____,

Statement of Proposed Executor's Compensation

Date: _____

1. Wages		
_____ hours @ $_____ per hour = _____ This represents _____ % of the net estate.	$	
Subtotal	$	$
2. Expenses		
$_____ out of pocket expenses	$	
_____ kilometres driven @ _____ per kilometre	$	
Subtotal	$	$
Total		**$**

Table 6
Time as Executor

Date	Hours Spent	Out-of-Pocket Expenses	Kilometres Driven	Details
2011-11-14	.75	$4.25		Went to bank to cash GIC and deposit funds into account. Paid for parking downtown.
2011-11-14		$0.50		Sent cheque to funeral home to pay bill. Paid postage.
2011-11-19	1.5		80	Went to house to hand over keys to buyer and walk through. Received cheque and put it in the account.
2011-12-16	10			Prepared financial statements. Sent to beneficiaries.
Totals	**12.25**	**$4.75**	**80**	

Once you have the totals, you can prepare your Statement of Proposed Executor's (or Administrator's) Compensation. In the example below, you can see how the numbers were transferred from your expenses records (such as in Table 6), which could be very lengthy, into a neat summary.

Use the following steps:

1. There is no standard hourly rate set by law for executors, but $20 an hour is considered reasonable, so that number has been used

in our sample. Multiply the number of hours you have spent by the rate you are charging and fill in your total. Remember that it is not required by law that you charge an hourly rate, so long as you do not exceed the range of 1 to 5 percent of the estate. If you choose, you can leave out the hourly calculation altogether and simply claim a percentage. However, breaking it down into an hourly rate is a good way to allow the beneficiaries to understand just how much work you did on the estate.

2. Transfer your total for wages into the right-hand column.

3. Calculate what percentage of the net estate (in our example, $406,110.27) is used up by your wage. Do not include your expenses in this calculation.

4. Fill in the total amount of your out-of-pocket expenses.

5. Fill in the total number of kilometres you have driven for the estate. Write in the amount you are charging per kilometre. There is no standard rate by law, but a good rule of thumb is not to exceed the amount being paid by the Alberta government to its employees. Multiply the kilometres by the rate and fill in the total.

6. Add together your out-of-pocket expenses and mileage costs and transfer that number to the right-hand column.

7. You now have an amount for wages and an amount for expenses showing in the right-hand column. Add them together to find the total amount you are claiming for executor's or administrator's compensation.

1. Wages		
12.25 hours @ $20 per hour	$245	
This represents less than 1 percent of the net estate		
Sub-total	$245	$245
2. Expenses		
Out-of-pocket expenses	$4.75	
80 kilometres driven @ 70¢ per km	$56	
Sub-total	$60.75	$60.75
Total		$305.75

4. Statement of Proposed Distribution

The Statement of Proposed Distribution is going to tie together the documents you have made so far. The purpose of this statement is to show the beneficiaries what is in the estate and how much each of them is going to inherit. Start with the current amount in the estate, list how much is needed for future taxes and expenses, then divide the rest among the beneficiaries. In the sample given below, we are continuing to use the numbers used so far in this chapter, and are assuming that there is a gift to a charity (Horse Heaven) of $5,000. There are also three residuary beneficiaries (Tom, Dick, and Harry). See Sample 45 and Table 7.

Use the following steps:

1. Fill in the name of the deceased and the date at the top.

2. Beside "Funds held in the estate," fill in the amount of money in the estate. This is the same number as the final balance shown in your Ledger/Statement of Receipts and Disbursements.

3. Under "Holdback for taxes," fill in the amount that you anticipate will be needed to pay any income tax that has not yet been paid. You may need to ask the person who prepared the income tax return for the estate how much this will be. Remember that it is better to overestimate than to underestimate. If all taxes are paid, put in "zero."

4. Under "Holdback for expenses," fill in the amount that you anticipate will be needed for any last-minute fees such as lawyers or accountants. This should not include your executor's or administrator's expenses, as you have already entered them in your Statement of Proposed Executor's Compensation.

5. Under "Executor's compensation," include the total amount from your Statement of Proposed Executor's Compensation.

6. From "Funds held in the estate," subtract the amounts for holdback and executor's compensation. In our sample, this would be $406,110.27 - 500.00 - 305.75 = $405,304.52.

7. The answer to this equation goes in the line next to "Funds available for distribution." This refers to money that is now available for you to give to the beneficiaries.

8. If there are gifts to specific beneficiaries, list them first.

9. Divide whatever is left in the estate among the residuary beneficiaries in the proportions indicated in the will or in Alberta's *Intestate Succession Act*. The amount that shows next to each beneficiary's

Sample 45
Statement of Proposed Distribution

In the Estate of _____

Statement of Proposed Distribution

Date: _____

FUNDS HELD IN THE ESTATE: $_____

    Holdback for taxes $_____
    Holdback for expenses $_____

    Executor's compensation $_____

FUNDS AVAILABLE FOR DISTRIBUTION: $_____

    To be paid to beneficiary 1 $_____
    To be paid to beneficiary 2 $_____

FUNDS THEN REMAINING IN ESTATE: NONE

name is the amount that eventually will be paid to them. It is a good idea to show the calculation of each share to head off questions from the beneficiaries. If this statement is properly set up, and if your supporting documents are also properly set up, your beneficiaries should be able to get a full picture of what is left in the estate and how much of it each of them will receive.

See Table 7 for an example of this math.

Table 7
The Math

FUNDS HELD IN THE ESTATE:		$406,110.27
Holdback for taxes	$500	
Holdback for expenses	$0	
Executor's compensation	$305.75	
FUNDS AVAILABLE FOR DISTRIBUTION:		$405,304.52
To be paid to Horse Heaven	$5,000	
To be paid to Tom (1/3 of $400,304.52)	$133,434.84	
To be paid to Dick (1/3 of $400,304.52)	$133,434.84	
To be paid to Harry (1/3 of $400,304.52)	$133,434.84	
FUNDS THEN REMAINING IN ESTATE:		NONE

5. Releases

You have now prepared all of the financial documents you need to report to the beneficiaries. Your next step is to get their approval so that you can send them their cheques. You do this by asking each to sign a release. The release is important to you as an executor or administrator because it protects you from any beneficiary who has signed one. It states that the beneficiaries will not ever come back against you for the transactions in your financial reporting.

The document is called a Form ACC12 Release. See Sample 46 for an example. You must prepare one for each residuary beneficiary. Preparing them for specific gifts such as the one to the charity in our example is optional and you may use your discretion.

Form ACC12 must be signed by the beneficiary in front of a witness. As you have seen with previous documents in this kit, this means that a Form NC11 must be attached to it for the witness to sign. Form NC11 is attached already for your convenience. Follow these steps to prepare both forms:

1. Fill in the court file number from your previous documents.

2. Fill in the judicial district from your Form NC1.

3. Fill in the estate name from your Form NC1.

4. Next to the word "Release," you will see that the form asks for a number. In almost all estates, there is only one round of release documents; therefore they are all called "#1." Unless you are doling out the estate in stages, you should fill in "1" here.

5. The period covered refers to the time period covered by your estate documents. Normally the start of the time period is the day that the deceased died. If this is the case, fill in "date of death." Otherwise, fill in a date.

6. The close of the time period will be the day that you send out the release. If you wish, you can fill in "date of release." Otherwise, fill in a date that corresponds to the last entry on your ledger.

7. Below the solid dividing line, you will fill in the name of the beneficiary as it shows on Form NC6 and his or her full address. Remember to make a separate release for each beneficiary.

8. There is no need to change anything in paragraphs 1 through 6.

9. In paragraph 7, you must choose whether the release you are sending out is an interim or a final release. It is almost always

Sample 46
Form ACC12

ACC12

COURT FILE NUMBER

COURT **Court of Queen's Bench of Alberta**
(Surrogate Matter)

JUDICIAL DISTRICT Edmonton

ESTATE NAME William Brown, a.k.a. Bill Brown

DOCUMENT **Release # 2**

PERIOD COVERED December 1, 2010 **to** December 31, 2011

This release has been signed by _____ Jillian Brown _____ of
(name of beneficiary)
_____ 111 Fifth Avenue, Calgary, Alberta T1T 1T6 _____ who is a person beneficially interested in
(full address of beneficiary)
the residue of the estate.

1. I have received from the personal representative(s) of the estate financial statements covering the period _____ December 1, 2010 _____ to _____ December 31, 2011 _____.

2. I approve the financial statements including the schedule of distribution and the schedule of compensation for the personal representative(s).

3. I understand that I will receive my share of the estate property as shown on the schedule of distribution, once the personal representative(s) have received releases from all the necessary beneficiaries.

4. If all the necessary beneficiaries do not sign a release, I understand that the personal representative(s) will apply for a court order approving the financial statements or dispensing with the need to pass accounts formally. The personal representative(s) will then distribute the estate property according to the order.

5. Until the financial statements have been approved by all concerned or by the court, my release will be held in trust.

6. In signing this release, I release and discharge the personal representative(s), their heirs, successors, personal representatives and assigns from any further claims by me against the estate and its property and against the personal representative(s) for their management and distribution of the estate to the date of this release.

7. This is a _____ final _____ release.
(final/interim)

_____ Jillian Brown _____
Signature of Beneficiary

_____ January 15, 2012 _____
Date

_____ I.M. Witness _____
Witness to signature of beneficiary

_____ J.B. Witness _____
Witness signature

a final one. It is only interim if you plan to send another in the future. Note that if you are holding back a small amount of the estate for taxes or expenses, you do not have to send another release in the future. Delete either "interim" or "final."

10. On Form NC11, fill in the estate name.

11. The "deponent" is the person who acted as witness for the beneficiary and who is now swearing to that. You probably will not know who this is and may leave it blank.

12. In paragraph 1, fill in the name of the beneficiary.

13. In paragraph 2, in the first blank fill in the name of the beneficiary. Leave the second blank empty.

14. You will notice that there are two versions of paragraph 3. Fill in the beneficiary's name in both of them.

15. In paragraph 4, fill in the beneficiary's name.

6. Sending the Documentation to the Beneficiaries

Once everything is ready, you will prepare a package for each beneficiary. Each beneficiary should receive the following:

- A letter explaining what to do
- Ledger/Statement of Receipts and Disbursements
- Statement of Proposed Executor's Compensation
- Statement of Proposed Distribution
- Form ACC12 Release (with Form NC11 attached)

The letter mentioned above is included in this kit on the CD. It contains instructions for the beneficiaries, which you should read in case they have questions. You do not have to send these by registered mail. You can use regular mail or courier. You can even email them if you like, as long as each beneficiary prints out Form ACC12 and Form NC11, signs them, and sends them back to you with the original signatures.

7. What to Do Once You Get Signed Releases

It is essential that you realize that NO beneficiaries may receive their cheques until ALL of them have returned their signed releases. Do not send out any cheques to anyone until you have received signatures from all the beneficiaries. Otherwise, you may find that someone is going to protest something that will have to be decided by the court, and by the time that happens, the estate will be smaller due to the amount of legal fees spent. Therefore, the amount due to each beneficiary will change and you will have to redo your Statement of Proposed Distribution.

When you have received all of the releases, you may send out the cheques to the beneficiaries in the amounts stated on the Statement of Proposed Distribution.

The releases are in a form that may be filed with the court on the estate file if you wish. It is not required by law. Filing the release with the court will create a permanent record of the beneficiary's approval of your actions. If you choose not to file them, make sure that you keep them somewhere safe so that if a beneficiary wants to dispute a financial transaction in the future, you can stop the dispute in its tracks with your documentation.

20

Distributing the Estate to Beneficiaries

You have reached the final step in the administration of the estate. In this chapter, we will look at the usual ways of giving the beneficiaries their shares of the estate. We will also look at some of the assets found in most estates. Always keep in mind that if the will gives specific details that differ from the general instructions given here, you must follow the instructions in the will.

There are some restrictions that an executor should keep in mind. Not every gift in a will can be carried out, particularly if the will was drawn up without the help of a lawyer. As noted in section **6.** below, you cannot give an inheritance to anyone under the age of 18 years. Read section **6.** for help in that situation. Also, a person cannot give away property that is jointly owned with someone else, because it is not his or hers to give away.

There are also gifts that are void. If a beneficiary was also a witness to the will, he or she cannot inherit something gifted in the will. The rest of the will is fine, but the item gifted to the witness must be treated as intestacy. This means you must distribute it according to the chart in Chapter 8.

Some gifts in wills are simply not enforceable. For example, gifts that are made on the condition that the beneficiary not marry her fiancé or never have children are not lawful. If the will you are distributing contains gifts like this or anything else unusual, it is a good idea to review the will with a lawyer before taking steps to pay out money.

All executors or administrators must transfer the assets of the estate to the beneficiaries (except in situations like those described in the previous paragraphs). As mentioned in Chapter 15, some assets must go through the step of being transmitted first. If you have already taken the steps outlined in Chapter 15 and have transmitted an asset into the name of the estate, this chapter will show you how to take the final step and give the asset to the beneficiary.

If you have to deal with complicated assets such as businesses or land in other countries, you should seek out the help of professionals. You may need a lawyer, trust company, or accountant to advise you.

You must pay specific gifts and give away household and personal goods before you divide the estate among residuary beneficiaries.

1. Six-Month Waiting Period

If you served a Form NC22, Form NC23, or Form NC24 notice on any beneficiary, you must wait six months from the date the court issues your grant of probate or grant of administration before you may give the beneficiaries their shares of the estate. This is because the people who received the notices have six months to start a claim against the estate. You are required by law to wait until that time is up to see whether anyone starts a lawsuit.

If everyone who was served with a Form NC22, Form NC23, or Form NC24 says in writing that they waive their right to make a claim against the estate, then you may choose not to wait the six months.

While you are waiting, you can get everything as ready as possible so that you are prepared to take the next steps as soon as the time is over. You can collect assets and deposit them into your executor's account. You can sell properties or other assets and put the funds into the account as well. You can also pay the funeral bill and any other liabilities, including loans and lines of credit that are outstanding. It is only the distribution of the estate to the beneficiaries that cannot go ahead during this time.

2. Household Goods

The term "household goods" usually includes anything located in the deceased's home, vacation property, cottage, garage, yard, shed, and workshop. Be careful with anything in a shop that the deceased used for work, as the contents may belong to someone else or form part of business assets.

Household goods normally include:

- Furniture, including linens
- Appliances
- Paintings and prints
- Wall decorations
- Musical instruments
- Electronics, computers, cameras, personal devices
- Books
- CDs and DVDs
- Photo albums
- Clothing
- Jewelry
- Collections (stamps, dolls, ceramics, coins, etc.)
- Antiques
- Tools
- Gardening equipment (hand tools, lawn tractors, etc.)
- Vehicles and accessories (trailers, covers, etc.)
- Consumables (food, wine, etc.)
- Plants and accessories
- Kitchenware, dishes, cutlery, etc.
- Souvenirs and mementos

Any money, savings bonds, or share certificates found in the house are not given away as personal goods. They are considered money of the estate and should be put into your executor's bank account.

Start by delivering any items that are specifically mentioned in the will, codicil, or memorandum. A memorandum is a handwritten list of items that are to be given to specific people. It is your responsibility to make sure that specifically-named items get to the person named. You can hand-deliver items, or you can mail or ship them. If the will or codicil mentions a memorandum or list, make a thorough search for it.

If the person named has already passed away, do not give the item to his or her family, but keep it as part of the estate. If the item to be given cannot be found, you cannot substitute another item in its place.

Check the will, any codicil, and any memorandum for instructions about who gets what. Sometimes wills contain instructions about drawing lots, or who chooses an item first. If so, you as the executor must use that method of sharing out the household and personal goods.

Keep a record of who takes which items (see Chapter 14 for detailed information on this topic as well as a form to use for recording the items).

If the will does not specifically mention household and personal goods, these items should be shared among the people who are named as residuary beneficiaries of the estate. Organize a day for everyone to meet at the house to go through and choose what they like. Do not give items to anyone other than residuary beneficiaries.

Once the residuary beneficiaries have taken the items they want, you can dispose of the rest of the household and personal items by using an estate auctioneer, a garage sale, or an online sale (for example, on sites such as eBay or Craigslist). All proceeds must go into your executor's bank account. If there are items left over that are not saleable, you may give them to a charity.

3. Specific Gifts

If the will directs you to pay a specific sum of money to a beneficiary, pay it out of your executor's bank account. Do not pay it from any other source. Always use a cheque or get a receipt so that you have a record of the payment.

If the will directs you to transfer a specific financial item such as a GIC or bank account, you may be able to transfer the asset without cashing it in. Before taking steps to cash it in, check with the bank to see whether the account or GIC can be transferred.

If the will directs you to give a vehicle to a beneficiary, use the pink registration slip to change the name on the vehicle at the registry. Make sure that registrations are properly done so that if the vehicle is later in an accident, the deceased's estate does not end up being involved. Also remember to advise the vehicle insurer once the vehicle has been transferred (and keep insurance on the vehicle while it is in the name of the estate).

4. Real Estate

If the will directs you to transfer a specific piece of real property to a certain beneficiary, you must first transmit the property from the deceased's name into the name of the estate. This process is described in Chapter 15. The Application for Transmission form is also discussed in that chapter.

You may wish to hire a lawyer to transfer the title to the beneficiary to ensure that the estate is fully protected. A lawyer will ensure that liens and encumbrances are cleared from the title, and can advise you on any financial or tax consequences to the estate that arise from the transfer.

If the real estate that is being transferred was the deceased's principal residence, there is no capital gains tax payable on the transmission to the estate or the transfer to a third party. If the property is not the principal residence, capital gains tax arises when the property is transmitted. The estate is responsible for paying those taxes, though the estate may not have the necessary funds until assets are sold.

5. Residue

The residue of an estate is made up of all assets that remain once all expenses and bills have been paid, the executor has been paid, and all specific gifts have been given to the beneficiaries. The residue is normally the largest part of an estate.

Read the will carefully to make sure you know who is supposed to get a share of the residue, and in what proportions. Check to see what you are supposed to do with the share of a beneficiary who has already passed away.

Normally when the executor is preparing to distribute the residue of the estate, he or she talks with the beneficiaries first. It can really help an executor to know ahead of time if any of the beneficiaries is interested in owing a specific asset. If so, that beneficiary can choose to have a certain asset — say the parents' home or an investment that is earning a good interest rate — rather than having the asset sold and receiving the money. Working out this kind of arrangement is a good idea, as it prevents disputes by beneficiaries who are disappointed if they do not receive a certain item.

If you are interested in making this kind of arrangement, check the wording of the will to make sure that the will allows it.

An issue that sometimes causes problems for executors and administrators is that of loans made by the deceased to his or her children during his or her lifetime. Most children who have received a loan will claim that the loan was a gift and was never meant to be repaid. However, the law states that unless the testator made it clear that a loan was to be forgiven, the executor has to treat the loan as if it were an advance on the child's inheritance. This means that a loan made to a child will reduce the amount that the child gets from the estate.

The executor will have to calculate how that loan affects the shares to the children. For example, Jack may have made a will in which he directs that his three children, Tom, Annie, and Walter, inherit his estate equally. His estate is worth $300,000. This would mean each child would get about $100,000. You read the will and find out that Jack did not ask that the loan of $30,000 he made to Tom be forgiven. Therefore, you take $30,000 off the share that Tom would otherwise get, which is the same as Tom repaying it. Then you divide the $30,000 among all of the children so that each gets an additional $10,000. The end result:

Annie:	$100,000	
	+ $10,000	
	$110,000	$110,000
Walter:	$100,000	
	+ $10,000	
	$110,000	$110,000
Tom:	$100,000	
	- (30,000)	
	$70,000	
	+ $10,000	
	$80,000	+ $80,000
		$300,000

Make sure that you use the financial reports as set out in Chapter 19 to show your calculations and proposed distribution to the beneficiaries before you actually pay out the money to them.

6. What to Do with Shares If Beneficiaries Are Minors

Children cannot inherit if they have not reached their 18th birthdays, so you cannot pay a minor child's share to him or her. You must set up a trust fund or trust account for each minor child at a bank or trust company.

Read the will to see if it gives instructions in this situation. It is common that testators give directions in the will about the following aspects of gifts to minors:

- The age at which the child is to inherit
- If the share is to be paid all at once or in staggered payments
- If the child is able to access the trust funds for certain purposes before his or her 18th birthday
- If a minor's share may be paid to a parent or guardian
- Any special conditions

As the executor or administrator of an estate, you are also the trustee of any trusts set up. While the share of a minor is being held in trust, you are responsible for making sure that the funds are properly invested in the best way and that they are paid out according to the terms set out by the will.

7. What to Do If Someone Has a Trustee

If any beneficiary of the estate has a court-appointed trustee or is being represented by an attorney under an Enduring Power of Attorney, you must deal with the trustee or attorney and not the beneficiary. If you are distributing a share of the estate in the form of cash, write the cheque to the trustee. For example, "John Smith, trustee for Janet Smith." Similarly, you may write a cheque to the attorney as "John Smith, power of attorney for Janet Smith."

8. Do Beneficiaries Pay the Cost of Getting Their Gift?

One general rule is that beneficiaries are entitled to receive the full value of the gift they were given. Another general rule is that all debts and expenses of the estate are paid from the residue of the estate. Together, these rules operate in such a way that a beneficiary does not have to pay to receive his or her inheritance.

For example, if a beneficiary is supposed to receive the deceased's house, the costs associated with the transfer of title — such as lawyer's fee or Land Titles Office fee — are paid out of the estate. The beneficiary gets the full value of the house.

Another common example arises when a gift to a beneficiary must be shipped to the beneficiary. This could be something like jewelry, heirlooms, or sentimental items. The item might be worth only $200, but it could cost $100 to ship it to the beneficiary. The $100 cost comes out of the estate, not out of the beneficiary's share, since the beneficiary gets the full $200 worth. If the item is something valuable that has to be insured, the cost of insurance is paid by the estate as well.

Read the will carefully before you follow this guideline. In a few wills, the testator has said that taxes or costs arising from a gift must be paid by a beneficiary. If the will does state this, it supercedes the general rule and the will must be followed. Although few wills contain this clause, you must check for it because it makes a huge difference to individual gifts.

9. Paying Gifts to Charities

If the will you are administering contains a gift to a charity, you must be absolutely sure that you pay the gift to the correct charity. If you pay it to the wrong one, you could be liable for paying the gift to the right one out of your own money.

Ideally, when the will was made, each charity was checked against the Canada Revenue Agency list of registered charities so that the correct name and registration number are contained in the will. Unfortunately not everyone takes that step, and even if they do, charities change over time as they close or amalgamate with others. It is up to you to determine the right charity.

The best way to ensure that the gift goes to the right place is to look it up on Canada Revenue Agency's list of registered charities. This list will give the proper name, the mailing address, and confirmation of whether the charity is still in good standing (see Sample 47).

If the gift to the charity is part of the residue of the estate, the charity is entitled to see the full accounting of the estate. When you gave the NC19 Notice to beneficiaries (residuary) at the beginning of your work as executor or administrator, you should also have included a copy of the full Application for Probate, including the will and Form NC7 Inventory of property and debt. If for any reason you have not given the charity those documents and they are entitled to receive a part of the residue, you should provide the documents along with the cheque.

Some gifts are expressed simply as a dollar amount, such as "I give $5,000 to Doctors Without Borders." Others may be expressed as a percentage, such as "I give 25 percent of my estate to the Stollery Children's

Sample 47
CRA Listing for a Charity

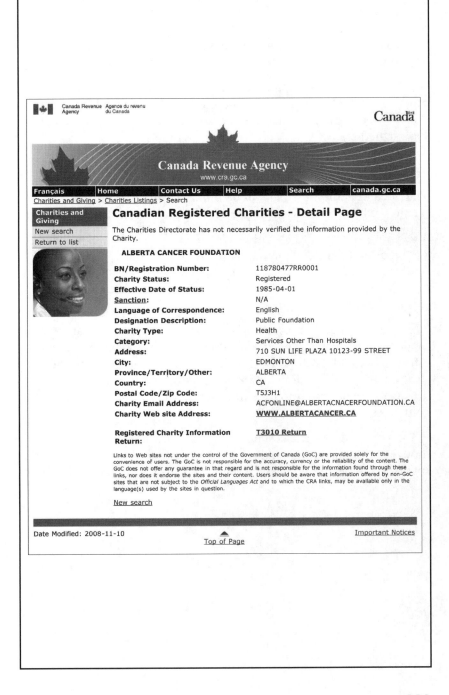

Canada Revenue Agency / Agence du revenu du Canada

Canada

Canada Revenue Agency
www.cra.gc.ca

| Français | Home | Contact Us | Help | Search | canada.gc.ca |

Charities and Giving > Charities Listings > Search

Charities and Giving

New search

Return to list

Canadian Registered Charities - Detail Page

The Charities Directorate has not necessarily verified the information provided by the Charity.

ALBERTA CANCER FOUNDATION

BN/Registration Number:	118780477RR0001
Charity Status:	Registered
Effective Date of Status:	1985-04-01
Sanction:	N/A
Language of Correspondence:	English
Designation Description:	Public Foundation
Charity Type:	Health
Category:	Services Other Than Hospitals
Address:	710 SUN LIFE PLAZA 10123-99 STREET
City:	EDMONTON
Province/Territory/Other:	ALBERTA
Country:	CA
Postal Code/Zip Code:	T5J3H1
Charity Email Address:	ACFONLINE@ALBERTACNACERFOUNDATION.CA
Charity Web site Address:	WWW.ALBERTACANCER.CA
Registered Charity Information Return:	T3010 Return

Links to Web sites not under the control of the Government of Canada (GoC) are provided solely for the convenience of users. The GoC is not responsible for the accuracy, currency or the reliability of the content. The GoC does not offer any guarantee in that regard and is not responsible for the information found through these links, nor does it endorse the sites and their content. Users should be aware that information offered by non-GoC sites that are not subject to the *Official Languages Act* and to which the CRA links, may be available only in the language(s) used by the sites in question.

New search

Date Modified: 2008-11-10

Top of Page

Important Notices

Hospital Foundation," or a fraction, such as "I give ½ of my estate to the Canadian Cancer Foundation."

When you are sending a cheque that you say represents the percentage or fraction of the estate the charity is entitled to receive, they have to be able to calculate whether you have sent the correct amount. Therefore, you have to send them your Statement of Receipts and Disbursements and your Statement of Proposed Distribution (explained in Chapter 19).

The charity should provide you with a signed release, just as any other residuary beneficiary would do. If the gift you send is a specified dollar amount and not a share of the residue, you may choose to not ask for a signed release.

10. Releases and Financial Statements

The documentation that should be in place before you pay out the estate to the beneficiaries is described in Chapter 19. Be sure to take care of these documents before you start distribution.

Once you have completed the distribution, your job as executor is done, at least for now. You are the executor of the estate for life, so if more assets are discovered in the future, you will have to take care of them as well.

As you can see, an executor's job is not simple. With care and attention to detail, you can certainly do it yourself. Remember to ask for information and assistance from those you encounter along the way, such as Land Titles Office clerks, Clerks of the Court, or the Public Trustee. They are used to executors acting without lawyers and can be goldmines of valuable tips.

If you find that the estate is much more complicated than you thought or is taking up much more of your time than you are able to spare, do not be afraid to ask for help from a lawyer or a trust company.